the cost of environmental protection:
regulating housing development in the coastal zone

CENTER
FOR URBAN
POLICY RESEARCH

The Cost of Environmental Protection

Regulating Housing Development in the Coastal Zone

Dan K. Richardson

CENTER FOR URBAN POLICY RESEARCH
RUTGERS – THE STATE UNIVERSITY OF NEW JERSEY
NEW BRUNSWICK, NEW JERSEY

About the Author:

Dan K. Richardson, previously a research associate at the Marine Sciences Center of Rutgers University, is now a member of the planning staff of the Office of Coastal Zone Management in the New Jersey Department of Environmental Protection and a Ph. D. candidate in geography at Rutgers.

Funding and Assistance:

This research was conducted under the auspices of the Marine Sciences Center, Rutgers University, under the sponsorship of the New Jersey Department of Environmental Protection with funding under the Coastal Zone Management Act of 1972 administered by the U.S. Department of Commerce, National Oceanic and Atmospheric Administration.

This study reflects the views and conclusions of the author and does not necessarily represent the views or policies of the Department of Environmental Protection of the State of New Jersey.

Library of Congress Cataloging in Publication Data:

Richardson, Dan K   1951-
    The cost of environmental protection.

    Bibliograph: p.
    1.   Coastal zone management—United States.   2.   Zoning —Economic aspects—United States.   3.   Housing—United States.   I.   Title.
HT392.R5   333.9'17'0973   76-2352
ISBN 0-88285-029-6

To
Maria Angelina
and
our parents

Contents

Illustrations

Tables:

Acknowledgments

The author would like to express his sincere appreciation and thanks to Dr. Norbert P. Psuty and Dr. Robert W. Burchell for their guidance and encouragement in carrying out this research. Special appreciation is extended to Dr. George Neiswand for his review; to Dr. George Sternlieb for his valuable discussion in the final stages of this work; to Lois Johnson for graphic design work; to Kathleen Agena and Carol Rosen for editorial services; and to John Frantz, Lydia Lombardi, Anne Hummel, and Liz Batchelder for typing the manuscript. Further thanks are in order to the personnel of the New Jersey Department of Environmental Protection for providing information and assistance; to officials of Dover Township and Ocean County, New Jersey for providing exceedingly detailed procedural, policy, and cost data; and to all the cooperating developers, engineers, consultants, and attorneys for their assistance during the field research.

Financial support for this study came from the coastal zone management program in the New Jersey Department of Environmental Protection, which is funded under Federal Grant No. 04-4-158-50028 by the Office of Coastal Management, National Oceanic and Atmospheric Administration, U.S. Department of Commerce. Additional support was received from the Marine Sciences Center and the Center for Urban Policy Research, Rutgers University.

D.K.R.

Chapter 1

Introduction

THE PROBLEM

The coastal zone has become a proving ground for attempts to coordinate various regulatory levels of land-use control. Since the turn of the century, the coastal zone has been subjected to steadily mounting development pressures and local land-use control efforts have not been equal to the task of either maintaining a viable coastal zone resource base or of resolving conflicting demands upon these resources. Thus, after nearly a decade of debate, the national government has formulated legislation which is designed to protect and manage the fragile coastal environment (Coastal Zone Management Act, 1972—P.L. 92-583). However, the federal legislation is primarily a mandate to the coastal states to develop and implement their own particular coastal zone management programs. Since a given coastal area might already fall under local and county land-use jurisdiction—and, perhaps, even regional controls—it would, under the federal legislation, be subject to state and national controls as well. Consequently, the regulatory process in such an area would be prone to unnecessary duplication and conflicting requirements; in other words, it could become an extremely inefficient and time-consuming procedure.

Inefficiency in the regulatory process and an increase in processing time are ultimately reflected in increased costs to the developer. If the development in question is a housing project, it is the housing consumer, according to Bosselman and Callies,[1] who will eventually have to bear the burden of inefficient, multilevel regulation in terms of increased housing costs. The impact of multilevel regulation on the price of local housing has been estimated but never empirically studied and never viewed with the idea that state and federally mandated controls might be integrated with local land-use regulations.* Most of the previous research examining the relationship between development controls and housing costs has concerned itself mainly with costs induced by zoning, housing, and building codes. Subdivision procedures and their accompanying regulations, bonding requirements, and authorizations have escaped sustained investigation. The emerging reality of state participation in environmentally oriented land-use decisions—which must operate within the context of local subdivision procedure—exists amidst acknowledged despair that empirical research examining the impact of relatively new environmental regulations might not become available for a considerable period of time.[2]

Today we are witnessing a pervasive failure of government agencies at all levels not only to adequately perceive their specific impact on land conversion procedures but to gauge the costs resulting from this impact as well. State agencies too frequently adopt the position that they will take no action in processing a development proposal until another agency has commented on an element of the proposal which falls within its substantive purview and local approvals have been obtained. Excesses in costs and processing time engendered by such a system have led March and others[3] to call for simultaneous state and local processing of development proposals.

The approach presently being used by many by coastal states, in an effort to obtain federal support for their costal zone management activities, is an interim permit procedure. In light of the growing trend toward state land-use regulation, there is a distinct possibility that these interim state review procedures will be permanently implemented. Thus, the potential pitfalls and costs of this procedure bear significance to an examination of regulatory costs for housing developments in the coastal zone.

In the coastal zone as in no other region has the "quiet revolution in land-use control"—the shifting of responsibility for land-use decisions to increasingly higher governmental levels and from private to public control—been so apparent, so active, and so confused. This

---

*The local land-use system is defined as the master plan, zoning, and subdivision ordinances. The plan describes how the community will be developed, according to what use and intensity of development, and by what levels of capital, infrastructure, and standards.

study is an attempt to analyze present regulatory procedures in the coastal zone, with an emphasis on the cost of these procedures to residential developers and housing consumers. It is hoped that such an analysis will prove beneficial to the various levels of government which are presently, or which will be, engaged in coastal zone management programs.

SPECIFIC FOCUS

Twenty-one residential developments in the Dover Township, New Jersey area were monitored from acquisition of land to final approval of the development proposal. The costs of obtaining each regulatory approval, including consulting engineering, legal, governmental fees, and holding costs incurred by the developer, were itemized. The costs of the regulatory process were then broken down according to costs incurred during the local regulatory process and those costs resulting from state intervention in that process.

In New Jersey, the Department of Environmental Protection (DEP) is responsible for administering the state coastal zone management program. At present, it is authorized under the New Jersey Coastal Area Facility Review Act (CAFRA) to regulate development of major facilities within the coastal zone by reviewing development proposals submitted to local-level coastal authorities. Originally, the CAFRA procedure took place after local regulatory processing. However, it was found that state entry at this point created an unnecessary delay in the regulatory process; therefore, the CAFRA review now begins during preliminary filing for a development and terminates prior to the bonding period for capital public works improvements. This shift in the point of state entry has decreased the total state-local regulatory process from thirty-three to twenty-four months for single-family developments and from twenty-eight to twenty-three months for multifamily developments. The cost incurred by a developer as a result of the standard regulatory process in New Jersey amounts to $4,584.00 per single-family unit and $2,185.00 per multifamily housing unit. As a result of the CAFRA procedure, these costs have now increased to $4,720.00 for single-family units and $2,310.00 for multifamily units—an increase of $136.00 for single-family housing units and $125.00 for multifamily units.

Of the $4,700 total costs for single-family developments, the initial cost of the land constitutes approximately $2,300 and regulatory costs $1,600 of the remainder. Thus, the original land investment of the developer is nearly doubled as a result of the regulatory process. A slightly lower ratio of land to regulatory costs applies for multifamily developments. Among the thirty some regulatory costs incurred by the developer, the costs related to the CAFRA review range among the largest. This study will focus on the relative significance of regulatory costs, with the idea that some of these costs might be minimized by combining or coordinating various regulatory procedures. The methodology for assessing processing time and costs, as well as a breakdown of these factors, is included in the discussion which follows.

The Dover Township coastal area lying, as it does, so close to the outer ring of the New York metropolitan region is subject to extreme development pressures and provides a realistic test-area for mechanisms intended to cope with multiple land-use conflicts in an area of fragile and limited natural resources.

NOTES

1. Bosselman and Callies, 1971, p. 319.
2. Bergman, 1975, p. 533.
3. Burgweger, 1975, p. 6; Blumenfeld, 1975, pp. 7-9; March, 1973, pp. 249-250.

Chapter 2

Coastal Development As A Growth Problem

THE COASTAL ZONE OF THE UNITED STATES

The lands and waters of the coastal zone* have been either mismanaged or not managed at all since the early settling of the United States. Though initial settlements were formed on coastal sites, the early settlers found that these sites were especially subject to natural hazards, and they soon abandoned them for more hospitable, inland areas. The coastal shorelands and islands were not extensively resettled until the late nineteenth century. Then, since the turn of the century, the trend from coastal development toward inland was reversed and the coastal zone is now experiencing population pressures (Figure 1) which threaten the future viability of many sections.[1]

Most of the metropolitan centers in the United States are located in coastal zones. Over half the nation's population, nearly 140,000,000 people, live in counties bordering the Atlantic and Pacific Oceans and Great Lakes shore. Statistics from the 1970 and 1973 censuses indicate that the migration from land-locked regions of the country to the seacoasts gained momentum during the 1960s. The thirty-one coastal and Great Lakes states currently contain more than 75 percent of the country's population. Estuarine regions within these states constitute only 15 percent of the states' lands but contain 33 percent of the coastal

---

*Roughly three longitudinal zones, open water, estuarines, and shorelands, are identified in the coastal zone. This study focuses on the shoreland strip of the coastal zone defined by the inland extension of marine influences. Suffice it to say at this point that the terms coastal zone and coastal area will be used interchangeably to refer to the shoreland zone subject to state coastal land use regulations.

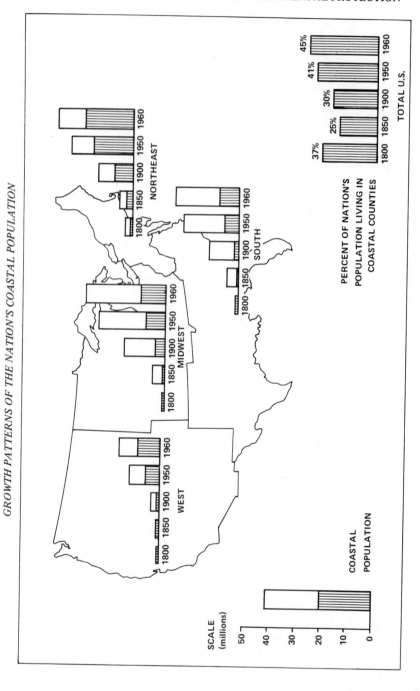

FIGURE 1

GROWTH PATTERNS OF THE NATION'S COASTAL POPULATION

states' population.[2] Furthermore, the coastal population is not equally distributed and it reflects the national trend toward urbanization. The seven largest metropolitan regions in the United States have significant portions of their areas within the coastal zone. The nation's most significant land and water transportation routes are found within coastal corridors. Heavy industrial complexes and their supporting services have sought coastal locations—lured by availability of land, labor, and water supplies. Commercial establishments, both convenience and nonconvenience variety outlets, are present in coastal areas. Finally, housing developments have sprung up in what were once remote, relatively inaccessible coastal areas. And massive landfill operations have covered valuable areas of the estuarine marshlands. All of these factors have contributed to the pollution and attendant degradation of the coastal waters.[3]

Pollutants transported down the rivers or in direct runoff from the land are concentrated within coastal estuarine systems and cause irreversible damage to the resources of the coastal interface.[4] In the long run, this condition will seriously affect the commercial fishing industry, 70 percent of which takes place in coastal waters at a yield of $300 million annually. The coastal estuarine waters and marshlands provide the nutrients, nursing areas, and spawning grounds for two-thirds of the world's entire harvest of fish, worth nearly $7.5 billion annually. These coastal estuarine areas may be even more important for aquaculture in the future, for they are among the most productive regions in the world. Estuarine areas, as shown in Figure 2, equal or double the production rates of the best upland agricultural areas and are fifteen to thirty times as productive as the open ocean.[5] The marine fisheries, which depend on the coastal zone, account for one-tenth of the world's animal-protein production and are one of the primary sources of food production.[6]

Land conversion and population settlement have led to extensive degradation of estuaries and marshlands in the coastal zone. Between 1922 and 1955, over one-fourth of the salt marshes in the United States were destroyed by filling, diking, or by constructing walls along the seaward marsh edge. Table 1 shows the distribution of the loss of estuarine environments among the coastal states from 1950 to 1970. More than one-half million acres, or 7 percent, of the fish and wildlife estuaries in the United States were dredged and filled during that twenty-year period.[7]

FIGURE 2

TERRESTRIAL AND MARINE PRODUCTION

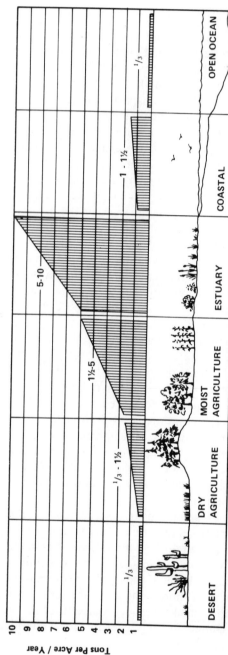

Comparative production rates among terrestrial and aquatic systems. Source: Redrawn from Teal and Teal, 1969, in "Man in the Living Environment", Report of the Workship on Global Ecological Problems, The Institue of Ecology, 1971

TABLE 1

ESTUARINE HABITAT AREAS LOST TO FILLING OPERATIONS
1950–1970

State	Total Area (Thousands)	Basic Area of Important Habitat (Thousands)	Area of Basic Habitat Lost by Dredging and Filling (Thousands)	Percent of Habitat Lost
		(Acres of Estuaries)		
Alabama	530	133	2	1.5
Alaska	11,023	574	1	.2
California	552	382	256	67.0
Connecticut	32	20	2	10.3
Delaware	396	152	9	5.6
Florida	1,051	796	60	7.5
Georgia	171	125	1	.6
Louisiana	3,545	2,077	65	3.1
Maine	39	15	1	6.5
Maryland	1,406	376	1	.3
Massachusetts	207	31	2	6.5
Michigan[1]	152	152	4	2.3
Mississippi	251	76	2	2.2
New Hampshire	12	10	1	10.0
New Jersey	778	411	54	13.1
New York State (Great Lakes)	49	49	1	1.2
North Carolina	2,207	794	8	1.0
Ohio[2]	37	37	2	.3
Oregon	58	20	1	3.5
Pennsylvania[2]	5	5	2	2.0
Rhode Island	95	15	1	6.1
South Carolina	428	269	4	1.6
Texas	1,344	828	68	8.2
Virginia	1,670	426	2	.6
Washington	194	96	4	4.5
Wisconsin[2]	11	11	2	.0
Total	26,618	7,988	569	7.1

1. In Great Lakes only shoals (areas less than 6 feet deep) were considered as estuaries.
2. Less than 500.

Source: Estuarine Areas, H.R. Rep. No. 989 to accompany H.R. 25, 90th Cong., 1st Sess., p. 8.

Note: Discrepancy in totals caused by rounding.

Housing developments have caused extensive damage in coastal zones. Those who produce or use housing are adept at overriding both natural and man-made environmental constraints and are seldom prevented from filling wetlands to produce marketable housing sites. Housing developments constitute the primary competitor for coastal zone resources and dominate the land use pattern within the coastal zone. A substantial amount of the estuarine environment has been lost to these developments, and they have produced significant pollution in the nearshore environment.[8] Even with the increase in offshore petroleum and mineral mining, the impact of housing remains the major source of coastal zone concern.

The Senate Committee on Commerce in its report to the U.S. Congress during consideration of the Coastal Zone Management Act of 1972 noted:

> The pressures of population and economic development threaten to overwhelm the balanced and best use of the invaluable and irreplaceable coastal resources in natural, economic, and aesthetic terms.
>
> To resolve these pressures . . . an administrative and legal framework must be developed to promote balance among coastal activities based upon scientific, economic, and social considerations. This would entail mediating the differences between conflicting uses and overlapping political jurisdiction.[9]

Well over one-half of the states have approved measures dealing with environmental problems.

The need for state land management expressed by the National Governors' Conference is also reflected in a survey of states, conducted by the Council of State Governments,[10] as shown in Table 2.

In their study of environmental problems in the coastal zone, Hite and Stepp pointed toward the need for federal as well as state regulations:

> Of all the natural resource-environmental policy problems facing the American people, the most pressing appear to be centered in the coastal zone. Coastal resources are not as widely scattered geographically as are other natural resources. They are concentrated in a rather narrow band where the continent meets the tidal sea, and they are used by a population scattered all across the continental land mass. The pressure on these scarce coastal resources has grown with increases in population, wealth, mobility, and leisure time. With this

TABLE 2

FACTORS GENERATING A NEED FOR STATE LAND
RESOURCE MANAGEMENT ACTION
(By percent of states expressing this factor)

		Percent
A.	Lack of adequate provision for future needs of:	
	1. Recreation	91
	2. Agriculture	72
	3. Residential communities	71
	4. Industry	70
	5. Forestry	57
	6. Business	48
B.	Inadequate Protection of:	
	1. Scenic areas	81
	2. Water supplies	79
	3. Historic areas	60
	4. Wildlife	59
	5. Estuarine and marine fisheries	58
	6. Despoliation caused by poor mining practices	42
C.	Lack of unified criteria upon which to measure developments proposed for critical areas	91
D.	Rapid uncoordinated and piecemeal development	90
E.	Parochial planning and zoning practices at the local level	79
F.	Lack of resources for adequate planning and zoning at the local level	74
G.	To provide for proper development of "new towns"	69
H.	Adverse developments contiguous to key public improvements and facilities	64

Source: The Council of State Governments, 1974, p. 34.

growing pressure has come increased conflicts over who is to use the
resources of the coastal zone, how they are to be used, and when that
use is to take place. The result has been a new interest at both federal
and state levels in devising a management system (or systems) for
the resources of the coastal zone. [11]

Certainly the importance of effective coastal zone management cannot
be over emphasized. Perhaps Dr. William Hargis, Vice-Chairman of
National Advisory Committee on Oceans and Atmosphere, has stated
it best:

> The coastal zone is the "key" or gate to the oceans. Effective
> management in the coastal zone almost automatically assures control
> over quality of ocean environment and quality of resources. [12]

FORMULATION OF A NATIONAL COASTAL ZONE MANAGEMENT PROGRAM

A coastal zone planning concept first emerged in coastal areas
where urban concentration adjoined large estuarine systems such as
Chesapeake Bay, Tampa Bay, Puget Sound, Narragansett Bay, and
San Francisco Bay. Plans were developed in an attempt to reconcile
conflicts between competing uses and their differential impact on the
natural resource base. Until the late 1960s, governments at all levels
examined or planned for a specific use in a limited area according to the
dictates of a particular set of circumstances. This approach proved to
be inappropriate in the coastal zone because no single demand of a
particular use could be satisfied without significant cost or denial to the
demands of other uses or to the resource base as a whole. [13]

Awareness of the potential crisis facing the nation's coastal zones
began to grow as early as the 1950s with the report of the National
Academy of Sciences Coordinating Committee on Oceanography. It
gained momentum in the mid-sixties through various committee reports and culminated in the Stratton Commission Report in 1969, which
recommended Congressional action to spur the formulation of a
federal-state system to manage the natural resources of the coastal
zone. The first steps toward a national coastal zone management program were taken by Congressman John O. Dingell (Michigan) who in-
troduced a bill (H.R. 13447) which was considered and rejected by the
Eighty-Ninth Congress. However, the Eighty-Ninth Congress did pass

the Marine Services Act (1966) which, among other things, mandated the Stratton Commission to look into potential problems affecting the coastal zone. Stimulated by that commission's report and growing state concern, the next three Congresses grappled with numerous proposals aimed at dealing with critical issues affecting the coastal zone.[14]

Congressman Dingell's renewed efforts in the Nintieth Congress met with more success than his initial attempt, largely due to a combination of the increased public sensitivity to environmental issues and the comprehensive planning efforts already underway in the urbanized estuaries. Dingell's bill H.R. 25 was subjected to lengthy and critical evaluation and, although the bill itself lacked a provision for a management system which weakened it to the point of virtual impotency, the deliberations surrounding the bill provided the foundation for further consideration of a coastal zone management program.[15]

With the Stratton report in hand, the Ninety-First Congress considered no less than seven bills, one even sponsored by the incumbent administration, all dealing with formulating a coastal zone management program. Beginning in late 1969 and continuing through 1970—during which time the National Oceanic and Atmosphere Administration (NOAA) was created—the process of hearing and redrafting coastal zone bills took place under the auspices of Senator Holling's Subcommittee on Oceanography. Early in the Ninety-Second Congress, a bill approved by the Subcommittee on Oceanography was forwarded to the Senate Committee on Commerce, altered slightly by other bills, and finally passed to the Senate. In the next session of Congress, the coastal zone bill was modified to: clarify jurisditional matters; limit coastal zone boundaries; and broaden interagency participation. Final hearings on the modified bill were held during April 1972, in the House Committee on Merchant Marine and Fisheries and the Senate Committee on Commerce. According to House Report No. 92-1049:

> The information developed during the course of the hearings on this legislation was remarkably consistent with the findings of all the predecessor groups that have considered the problem. Witnesses representing the National Governor's Conference, the National Legislative Conference, the Coastal State's Organization, individual state governments, and various conservation and public interest groups, were uniformly concerned for the deteriorating condition of the coastal zone and were united in their support for early legislative action.

The Ninety-Second Congress did act promptly on the coastal zone management bill, but one last hurdle remained before the legislation could be forwarded to the White House. Both the Department of Interior and NOAA had been proposed at one time or another to administer the program. The Senate-House conference had designated NOAA to administer the program. The conference committee finally convinced the House of Representatives that NOAA was the sole agency with the necessary technical expertise to administer the bill. Congressional approval came in the early fall and the President signed the Coastal Zone Management Act (P.L. 92-583) into law on October 27, 1972.

This act is the first and only comprehensive land-use control legislation to be passed by Congress. It is not intended to be simply another categorical planning effort supported by the federal government. States are encouraged to exercise their authority not only through funding incentives but also through exerting limited control over federal activities which fall within their coastal zones. The act also provides several ways in which local and regional interests can be taken into account in the preparation and implementation of such a program. With the clear designation of the state government as the central actor in this land use control process, the act represents a considerable challenge to traditional concepts of local autonomy in the control of land use.

After delays in funding, the NOAA's Office of Coastal Environment—later to become the Office of Coastal Zone Management—began administering the program in early 1974. Nearly $12 million were appropriated, on a two-thirds federal and one-third state matching basis, for the first year of the program. Of the thirty-four eligible states and territories, thirty-one initially participated. By the second year, all coastal states were developing management programs to deal with problems of their coastal zones.

PROVISIONS FOR RESOURCE MANAGMENT

The fundamental requirement of the Coastal Zone Management Act is that each state must demonstrate a commitment to manage its coastal zone on both a coordinated and comprehensive basis. The states are eligible for federal funding under the act if they attempt to fulfill the following objectives:

1. An intent to increase the level of consciousness of all levels of government regarding the importance of the resources of the coastal zone, and the need for their balanced management;
2. Understanding and articulation of the impact of various uses especially the short and long term consequences of such impacts on the coastal zone;
3. An attempt to minimize adverse impacts; and
4. The necessity of broadening and diversifying the decision-making process to include the full range of those affected by management decisions.

Coastal states are free to choose among several management program alternatives designed to suit their particular set of circumstances.[16] The act defines a management program as:

> a comprehensive statement in words, maps, illustrations, or other permanent media of communication . . . setting forth objectives, policies, and standards to guide and regulate public and private uses of the lands and waters in the coastal zone.[17]

In the administration of this federal program it is emphasized that coastal zone management is more than a simple articulation of policies and management approaches. Instead, management of the program must include a set of procedures and institutional arrangements to carry out the established policies. The requirements of the act focus on the process of management and, although basic guidelines are provided, the act leaves the substance of the management programs to the discretion of the individual state. Federal grant programs are established by the act to assist states in the process of program development (Section 305) and the process of implementation and management (Section 306). The act also authorizes expenditures for the acquisition of estuarine sanctuaries on a matching-fund basis.

> In sum, the act brings the federal government into an overseeing role, designates the states as the focal points for action in the development of effective coastal zone management programs, and urges the states to build local governmental competence and interest into their programs.[18]

The guidelines of the Coastal Zone Management Act structure the process of program development through the establishment of various elements which states must consider when formulating their coastal zone management programs. NOAA, the administering federal agency, requires states to define coastal boundaries, determine permissible uses, identify geographic areas of particular concern, and establish the priority of uses in their coastal areas. Beyond these substantive planning tasks, NOAA emphasizes the need for information dissemination, public participation, and most importantly, establishing adequate state authority to implement the program. In combination, these elements of the program development process provide each coastal state with a means of producing a range of alternative management strategies during the formulation of its management program.

Designation of the State Lead Agency

The first task for states participating in the federal coastal zone program is to designate an agency to administer the program. Planning, environmental protection, and natural resource departments have been the most frequently designated agencies to date.[19] Many of the states had to reorganize in order to create an agency with the authority and capability to implement the federal program.

Boundary Delineation

The next order of business for the states is usually delineation of coastal zone boundaries. Three longitudinal zones—open water, estuarine, and shorelands—are identified in the coastal zone, each presenting its own particular problems of delineation. In establishing boundary guidelines, the existing limits of natural systems, jurisdictional units, and social neighborhoods, and the interrelationships between these must be taken into account. It is also suggested that a larger planning area than is typically covered under municipal or county designations should be utilized in order to provide an indication of impacts existing outside the specific coastal area.

In the past, a few coastal states proposed boundaries which they had established prior to adoption of the Coastal Zone Management Act. These states then updated and expanded their methods of determining boundaries in order to include cultural features, natural features, jurisdictional units, demographic units, and distance offsets from baselines. Examples of each technique may be found, respectively, in New Jersey and Delaware, Oregon, Texas, Florida, and California and Wisconsin.[20]

Designation of Critical Areas—Permissible Uses

Designation of permissible uses, critical areas, and the priority of uses is usually based upon a natural resource inventory taken within the confines of the coastal planning area. Determination of coastal land and water uses and designation of the methods for assessing their impact on the coastal environment provides the basis for the eventual formulation of a state's coastal zone management strategies. There are three types of inventory and mapping programs for the coastal zone. In order of sophistication, they are: (1) single factor maps; (2) designation of environmental/socioeconomic units; and (3) systems delineation based upon the interaction among the various units. New Jersey, Washington, Alaska, Oregon, Maine, Florida, Delaware, and Texas all employ the single-factor map technique as at least one element of their environmental inventory. The land and water resource capability units developed in Texas illustrate environmental/socioeconomic designations, whereas the programs of Maine and Louisiana represent the system delineation approach.

Various portions of nearly every state's coastal zone are subjected to one or more inventories or analyses prior to designation—inventories of uses, local comprehensive planning, single-purpose mapping, coastal dependency/inland alternative determinations, input-output analyses, and so forth. Overlays and comparisons of two or more of these several inventory and analysis techniques define the nature, location, scope, and conflicts of current and future land uses. The classification of coastal areas may then be used as a legal rationale for the designation of permissible uses, critical areas, and priority uses.[21]

The uses permitted in a state's coastal zone are essentially those remaining after a two-stage sifting process has taken place. First, specific uses are excluded from the entire zone and, second, certain types of generally permissible uses are removed from particular coastal environments or specific geographic areas where they would be more detrimental than in other parts of the zone. Critical areas are those which have the potential of being depleted of their resources—that is, locations where projected demand exceeds the available resource base or areas in which the resource base is unnaturally limited or unique. Eight types of geographic areas of particular concern are designated in the Coastal Zone Management Act (Section 305):

1. areas of unique, fragile, or vulnerable natural habitat;
2. areas of high natural productivity or essential habitat;
3. areas of substantial recreational value;
4. areas where activities are dependent upon coastal waters;
5. areas of unique geologic or topographic significance to industrial or commercial development;
6. areas of urban concentration;
7. areas of significant hazard, if developed; and;
8. areas needed to protect, maintain or replenish coastal lands or resources.

Priority of Uses

The priority of permissible uses within the coastal zone is partially determined by the state's classification of critical areas. Beyond this, the priority of uses is determined on the basis of existing commitment of land, control of surrounding land use, impacts of use on surrounding areas, scarcity and uniqueness of the natural environment, diversity of location, irreversible commitments of resources, dependency on coastal location, economic efficiency/social equity considerations, regional benefits and national interests, fair-share responsibilities and/or public preference, and, finally, the ability to implement a designated use.

Whereas boundaries and permissible uses are usually applicable to the entire coastal zone, a tandem of policies are involved in the designation of critical areas and priority uses. The designation of critical areas and priority uses may reflect a "continuous" planning policy which covers the entire coastal area, as in Texas, or a "scattered" policy, as in Massachusetts, where the designations effect only specific portions of the coastal zone. Whatever criteria is devised or approach adopted, all four elements—boundaries, permissible uses, critical areas, and priority uses—must be addressed by the coastal state during the process of program development.

Information System Development

The development of research and technical information systems is also an integral component of the coastal zone management program. Decisions regarding boundaries, permissible uses, critical areas, and priority uses rely heavily upon the data derived from coastal zone inventories. While to date, the emphasis has been on gathering *existing* information, additional research is frequently necessary to supplement the existing data base. Information tabulated by coastal states typically is drawn from documents,[22] maps with data,[23] or a combination of both. State information agencies are charged by the federal legislation with providing relevant and up-to-date information to coastal zone administrators. One of the goals of the coastal zone management program is to establish a data storage and retrieval system for continuous monitoring of activities in the zone. The specific mechanics of developing information systems has been left to the individual states.

Public Participation

Federal legislation stresses public participation in the state coastal zone management program to ensure the viability of the program, improve the efficiency of economic transactions, foster social equity, and control the influence of special interests. In accordance with the act's intent to broaden and diversify the planning process to involve a spectrum of those affected by management decisions, mandatory rule-making public hearings are specified and special forums to solicit the views of all groups are encouraged. A trio of public participation techniques are commonly utilized in the coastal zone program. These follow the suggested format by the National Environmental Protection Act (1970) and consist of public hearings, informal exchange and circulation of information, and citizen review and advisory boards. Nearly every coastal state and territory employs some form of each of these participatory mechanisms to create a climate of collaborative planning for formulating its management programs. In addition, advocacy planning, public opinion surveys, and individual feedback may further the information flow which is crucial to participatory planning.[24]

Implementation and Regulation

Federal reviews of initial state requests for program approval have focused on a state's ability to implement the coastal zone management program.[25] The administrative organization and authority of the state to implement a coastal zone management program are considered the most crucial elements of the national effort to deal with the crisis in the coastal zone. Under the Coastal Zone Management Act (Section 306), each coastal state must select one or a combination of up to three management approaches: (1) a state may establish criteria and standards for local implementation, but it must retain responsibility for administrative review and compliance enforcement; (2) responsibility for planning and regulation of land and water uses may be assumed exclusively by the state; and (3) while allowing local authorities to retain control, a state may review all local plans, projects, or regulations in terms of their consistency with the statewide plan. In most cases, one or a combination of these approaches divides the authority to regulate coastal zone resources between a state agency and substate units already involved in land and water regulation. Whichever administrative approach a state selects, only one state agency may be delegated final authority for coastal zone management.

The lead coastal zone management agency in the state must have the authority to coordinate all public and private activities in the coastal zone. Administrators in the agency must have open access to the state's chief executive and significant regulatory powers to allocate coastal resources effectively.[26] As shown in Table 3, states such as Alaska, Connecticut, Maryland, Massachusetts, New Jersey, and Pennsylvania have designated "super-agencies" to fullfill nearly all of the federal prerequisites. In most coastal states, however, (including Delaware, Georgia, Hawaii, Illinois, Louisiana, Maine, Minnesota, New Hampshire, New York, North Carolina, Ohio, and Rhode Island) a less comprehensive agency has been designated to administer the coastal program. Finally, a few states have created new agencies and separated the coastal zone management program from other state functions. California's Coastal Zone Conservation Commission and Florida's Coastal Coordinating Council are leading examples of this approach. Alabama, Mississippi, Oregon, and South Carolina have also created special coastal agencies.

As noted previously, the organizational structure to implement the coastal zone management program has primarily two levels, state and local, with some states proposing an intervening county or regional administrative level. The state's control over the allocation of coastal resources obviously depends upon intergovernmental cooperation between municipal and state political subdivisions. Whereas the act (Section 305) presents three regulatory alternatives, recognition of the local power base in land-use control suggests state dependency upon the third approach, with the promulgation of standards for local im-

TABLE 3

STATE ORGANIZATIONS FOR COASTAL ZONE MANAGEMENT, 1974

State	Lead Agency	Type of Organization
Alabama	Alabama Development Office	special agency
Alaska	Department of Environmental Conservation	super agency
California	California Coastal Zone Conservation Council	special agency
Connecticut	Department of Environmental Protection	super agency
Delaware	State Planning Office	coordinating agency
Florida	Coastal Coordinating Council (DNR)	special agency
Georgia	Office of Planning and Budget	coordinating agency
Hawaii	Department of Planning and Economic Development	coordinating agency
Illinois	Department of Conservation	coordinating agency
Louisiana	State Planning Office	coordinating agency
Maine	State Planning Office	coordinating agency
Maryland	Department of Natural Resources	super agency
Massachusetts	Executive Office of Environmental Affairs	super agency
Michigan	Department of Natural Resources	super agency
Minnesota	State Planning Agency	coordinating agency
Mississippi	Marine Resources Council	special agency
New Hampshire	Office of Comprehensive Planning	coordinating agency
New Jersey	Department of Environmental Protection	super agency
New York	Office of Planning Services	coordinating agency
North Carolina	Department of Natural and Economic Resources	coordinating agency
Ohio	Department of Natural Resources	coordinating agency
Oregon	Land Conservation and Development Commission	special agency
Pennsylvania	Department of Environmental Resources	super agency
Puerto Rico	Department of Natural Resources	coordinating agency
Rhode Island	Department of Administration	coordinating agency
South Carolina	Coastal Zone Planning and Management Council	special agency
Texas	General Land Office	coordinating agency
Virginia	Division of State Planning and Community Affairs	coordinating agency
Washington	Department of Ecology	coordinating agency
Wisconsin	Department of Administration	coordinating agency

Source: Derived from assorted information in Haskell and Price, 1973, pp. 268-271; and Office of Coastal Zone Management, 1974.

plementation and state administrative review and permit procedures. Exclusive state control is out of the question, in most cases, given the political realities of home rule. However, allotting a state agency the authority to grant permits on major projects and review local plans may well be sufficient to carry out the act's charge.

Either of two relationships between the state and local governments may be employed to properly implement a management program in the manner prescribed in the Coastal Zone Management Act. One is a relationship in which both state and substate units have similar, generally defined functions, including coastal protection mandated by statewide land use enabling legislation establishing conforming local land-use ordinances. The other relationship is hierarchical—the function and authority of coastal agencies at all levels are specifically linked by statute or executive order. In essence, in either of these administrative approaches, the range of control for coastal land and water uses must be defined for each governmental level and agency, and the interactive processes between governments must monitor the incremental commitments of coastal resources.

The effectiveness of the coastal zone management program hinges directly upon the ability of the states to translate the legislative mandates and guidelines of the Coastal Zone Management Act into programs which deal directly with the problems of population pressure and the criticality/priority of competing uses. Though a sound basis for decision making can develop from the designation of permissible uses, critical areas, and priority of uses, and the completion of environmental inventories, it is the legal and administrative framework of the program that determines how well the nation, through its states, resolves the crisis in the coastal zone.

THE NEED FOR RESEARCH

The Focus of this Study

In order to create an effective program of coastal zone management, much more is required than the mere coordination of mandated program activities and existing land use law. Armstrong has recommended that:

. . . states . . . consider operational or behavioral studies as a technique to measure a law's effectiveness. Surveys or interviews with coastal users and regulators could reveal how current administrative programs are working day-to-day, as well as reveal major strengths and weaknesses of regulatory programs. A combined legal and operational assessment would provide a sounder base from which a state could develop new laws or modify existing ones.[27]

The question is not only what mechanisms are available to regulate coastal activities, but, in addition, what impact these mechanisms will have. Agencies at each level of government typically develop rules and regulations outlining their particular administrative jurisdictions, but they know precious little about the combined regulatory process in which they collectively participate. It would, therefore, seem highly advantageous to analyze the effects the various controls would have prior to their implementation. Such an analysis would be particularly beneficial for agencies regulating the coastal zone. Without clarifying the impact of various administrative alternatives for managing the coastal zone, states risk legitimizing procedure rather than control and, by so doing, create a climate of avoidance rather than acceptance.

The impact of state regulation upon the local regulatory processes is certainly one effect of control that should be analyzed. However, in the area of environmental regulation, this remains a largely uncharted area. The integration of state major facilities permitting into the local regulatory process especially needs more extensive analysis. This study seeks to provide insight into the impact of state major facilities permitting and to examine this process in light of the overall operation of national land-use programs.

The Focus of Comparable Research

State land use regulation is a relatively recent phenomenon. Consequently, research which examines the impact of state regulation on local administrative procedures is rather scarce. (Table 4 classifies the standard environmental regulations in terms of effectiveness; Table 5 illustrates environmental performance zoning mechanisms; Table 6 presents various permit mechanisms in effect in coastal states.) One study, "Coastal Policy Development and Self-Evaluating Agencies: Information Utilization and the South Coast Regional Commission," by Rosentraub and Warren, summarizes an empirical analysis of the permitting activities of the most active coastal commission in

THE COST OF ENVIRONMENTAL PROTECTION

TABLE 4

REGULATORY TOOLS LISTED IN ORDER OF EFFECTIVENESS
IN ACHIEVING ENVIRONMENTAL QUALITY
(Most effective are at top of the list)

Type of control (% of agencies using it)	Percentage of Respondents using the tool and rating the tool as:			
	Very Effective	Moderately Effective	Slightly Effective	Not Effective
Most Effective				
Burning ordinance (68%)[1]	46	36	16	2
Burying utility lines reg't. in subd. ordinance (48%)	43	39	16	1
Subdivision regulations generally–(86%)	34	46	18	2
Planned water and sewer reg's. of subd. regs. (75%)	45[2]	31	20	4
Flood plain zoning (42%)	40	35	24	2
Less Effective				
Conservation easements (13%)	29	48	24	0
Historic preservation controls (24%)[3]	32	41	27	0
Marshland controls (19%)	33	58	3	6
Historic district zoning (23%)	29	41	29	0
Effluent ordinances (47%)	33	58	3	6
Health/sanitation ordinances (78%)	32	44	22	3
Special district zoning, generally (32%)[4]	21	60	17	2
Density zoning (57%)	27	47	24	2
Dedication of open space reg'ts. of subd. regs. (58%)	33	37	25	5
Preservation of trees reg'ts. of subd. regs. (37%)	31	37	26	6
Performance standards (43%)	23	53	18	6
Emissions ordinance (46%)	25	51	19	6
Tree ordinance (25%)	19	48	31	2
Utility & other easements (66%)	35	33	21	11
Sedmentation/erosion controls (25%)	13	54	33	0
Building ordinance (83%)[5]	30	34	26	9
Least Effective				
Large lot zoning (2+ acres) (32%)[6]	22	50	20	9
Excavation controls (49%)	17	45	36	3
General zoning ordinance (90%)	14	56	26	5
Appearance ordinance (13%)[7]	9	50	41	0
Sign ordinance (72%)	15	43	36	6
Special use/variance mechanisms (84%)	21	41	25	14
Agricultural zoning (40%)[8]	18	32	36	15
Housing codes (73%)	12	50	26	12
Noise ordinance (30%)[9]	13	23	47	17
Litter ordinance (57%)[10]	11	38	40	11

1. Principal cities of SMSAs much more likely to use a burning ordinance (88%); and counties much less (46%).
2. Municipalities in SMSAs more likely to rate public water and sewer requirements within subdivision regulations as a very effective tool.
3. Principal cities of SMSAs more than twice as likely as others to use historic districting (47%) and historic preservation controls (56%).
4. Principal cities of SMSAs twice as likely to use special district zoning (56%) vs. 20 to 30%).
5. Municipalities in SMSAs more likely to use building ordinances (95%) than other jurisdictions.
6. Municipalities in SMSAs much less likely to use large lot zoning (10%) vs. 50% for other agency types.
7. Non-principal cities in SMSAs are 3 times as likely to use appearance controls (28%) vs. 8% for other agency types.
8. Municipalities in SMSAs less than half as likely to use agricultural zoning (20% vs. 50%).
9. Municipalities in SMSAs more than twice as likely to use noise ordinances (45% vs. 18% for other agency types).
10. Principal cities of SMSAs more likely to use litter ordinances.

Note: Order has been determined by considering the percentage of responses in "very effective" category, number in "very effective" plus "moderately effective" categories, and percentage of responses in "not effective" category.

Source: Kaiser *et al.*, 1974, pp. 84-85.

TABLE 5

PERFORMANCE ZONING IN RESOURCE MANAGEMENT
AS APPLIED TO A FIFTY ACRE TRACT

Resource	Recommended Open-Space Ratio	X	Area Mapped (Acres)	=	Area Needed to Protect the Resource (Acres)
Floodplains	1.00		10		10
Alluvial Soils	1.00		0		0
Lakes, Ponds, Watercourses	1.00		5		5
Wetlands	1.00		0		0
Prime Agricultural Soils	.85		0		0
Pond Shores	.80		0		0
Lake Shores	.70		10		7
Forests	.70		10		7
Steep Slopes					
8 to 15%	.60		10		6
15 to 25%	.70		5		3.5
25% or more	.85		0		0
Total			50		38.5

Source: Frank, 1975, pp. 4-5.

TABLE 6

COASTAL STATES PERMITTING MECHANISMS, 1975

State	Shore-line Zoning	Major Facilities[1]	Wet-lands	Flood-plains	Dredge and Fill	Shore-land Uses	Other[2]
Alabama		X					X
Alaska		X	X				X
California			X		X	X	X
Connecticut			X		X		X
Delaware		X	X		X		X
Florida		X	O		X		X
Georgia			X		X		
Hawaii	X						State Zoning
Illinois	X			X			X
Louisiana				X			X
Maine	X						X
Maryland		X	X				X
Massachusetts			X				X
Michigan		X				X	X
Minnesota	X				X		X
Mississippi			X				X
New Hampshire			X				X
New Jersey		X	X	X			X
New York		O	X		X		X
North Carolina		X					X
Ohio							X
Oregon		X					X
Pennsylvania				X	X		X
Puerto Rico	X				X		X
Rhode Island		X	X				X
South Carolina			O				X
Texas					X		X
Virginia			X				X
Virgin Islands						X	X
Washington	X	X					X
Wisconsin	X			X			X

1. Definitions vary among states.
2. Includes many types of permits pertaining to air, water, noise, solid waste, pesticides, and radiation pollution.

Note: X denotes operational mechanisms; O denotes pending mechanisms.

Source: Office of Coastal Zone Management, 1974; Burchell & Listokin, 1975, pp. 14-36; Haskell & Price, 1973, pp. 268-271; and state first year grant proposals.

California, the South Coast Regional Commission. Among its several thrusts, the study monitors the application-to-decision turn-around times for the equivalent of the New Jersey procedures. As shown in Table 7, the monthly tabulations of the time period between application and final decision provide a clear indication that state permitting procedures do not necessarily require less time as the agency gains administrative experience. In fact, quite the contrary is indicated. As the agency gained experience, it took more time to process proposals for major residential projects. Whereas it took four months or more to process only 30 percent of the major residential projects in the first year of the program's operation, the following year, 1974, saw nearly 80 percent of these developments subjected to at least four months of review. A word of caution regarding this observation is in order. The information may also be interpreted as the result of increased scrutiny being applied to reviewing permits during the tremendous slump in development activity in the second year. Whatever the reason for the shift toward longer processing time, the trend is not an encouraging one.

The research conducted in California is not directly applicable to New Jersey, because an extensive environmental impact statement review is not a mandatory part of California's permit procedure and, furthermore, processing time-limits are not comparable for the various stages of permit review. Taking into account these variations in a comparison of the California experience with that of New Jersey (as indicated in Table 8), approximately six months must be added to the decision periods in California to reflect the procedure in New Jersey. This adjustment, however, does not alter the observable trend toward longer review periods. Nevertheless, it should be noted that the Rosentraub and Warren study reflects the time period from application to the decision date, whereas this study will examine the time period from application to issuance of the permit. The latter time-frame better reflects the actual delay posed by the state review process on local development.

Although there is a significant amount of literature about the impact or regulatory procedures on housing costs, it is almost always of a theoretical nature. Empirical studies which examine the specific impact of developmental controls on housing costs are extremely rare. Edward M. Bergman, in "Development Controls & Housing Costs: A Policy Guide to Research," reported only twelve such studies in this field.[28] Of the twelve, few examined the costs associated with either

TABLE 7

PERMITTING PERIODS
SOUTH COAST REGIONAL COMMISSION[1]
LOS ANGELES, CALIFORNIA

Month/ Year	Projects Proposed[3]	Time Required to Decision (Months)[2]				
		One	Two	Three	Four or more	No Action[4]
3/73	3	–	3	–	–	–
4/73	9	–	7	2	–	–
5/73	7	–	1	5	1	–
6/73	15	3	1	6	5	–
7/73	14	2	2	6	4	–
8/73	3	1	–	1	1	–
9/73	4	–	1	–	3	–
10/73	5	–	1	2	2	–
11/73	3	–	1	1	1	–
12/73	4	–	–	1	3	–
1/74	7	–	–	–	–	7
2/74	3	–	1	–	–	2
3/74	0	–	–	–	–	–
4/74	1	–	–	–	–	1
5/74	0	–	–	–	–	–
6/74	5	–	1	–	3	1
7/74	1	–	1	–	–	–
8/74	2	–	–	–	1	1
9/74	6	–	1	1	4	–
10/74	6	–	–	–	6	–
11/74	3	–	–	1	2	–
12/74	1	–	–	1	–	–
1/75	3	–	–	–	–	3
1973	67	6	17	24	20	0
1974	35	0	4	3	16	12

1. One of six regional commissions established in 1973 to administer an interim permit mechanism in areas within 1,000 yards of the California coast.
2. Major residential projects consisting of 26 units or more.
3. At least 91 percent of projects listed required public hearing.
4. Those projects classified "no action" may be considered to have at least four-month processing periods since the most recent entry is from August, 1974.

Source: Derived from assorted information in Rosentraub and Warren, 1975.

TABLE 8

STATE OF NEW JERSEY[1]
CAFRA PERMITTING PERIODS

Month/ Year	Residential[3] Projects Proposed	Time Required to Decision (Months)[2]					
		2-4	5-7	8-10	11-13	14-16+	Pending or Cancelled[4]
10/73	1	—	1	—	—	—	—
11/73	2	—	—	2	—	—	—
12/73	3	2	—	1	—	—	—
1/74	4	1	—	—	1	—	2
2/74	5	1	!	-	1	1	1
3/74	4	—	1	—	2	1	—
4/74	6	—	1	2	2	1	—
5/74	3	—	1	1	—	1	—
6/74	6	—	—	2	1	2	1
7/74	6	—	1	2	—	—	3
8/74	4	—	—	1	1	1	1
9/74	1	—	—	1	—	—	—
10/74	2	1	—	—	—	—	1
11/74	7	1	—	1	2	1	2
12/74	3	—	—	2	—	—	1
1/75	5	1	1	—	1	—	2
2/75	2	—	—	1	—	—	1
3/75	2	—	—	1	—	—	1
4/75	5	—	2	—	—	—	3
5/75	2	—	2	—	—	—	—
6/75	2	1	—	1	—	—	—
7/75	7	—	1	—	—	—	6
Total	82	8	12	18	11	8	25

1. Add at least 2 months to each project to reflect typical time interval proceeding actual issuance of permit.
2. Major residential projects proposing 25 units or more.
3. All projects require a public hearing and EIS.
4. This table is indicative of the 12 month timeframe utilized in this study to characterize processing times; few pending projects submitted since 12/74 have had the public hearings as of 8/1/75. An additional three months commonly elapse between hearing and decision with another one or two months required to issue the permit.

Source: Division of Marine Services, Department of Environmental Protections, State of New Jersey.

the subdivision process or state permit-review process. The exception, *Zoning and Housing Costs* (1973) by Lynne B. Sagalyn and George Sternlieb, provided a basic format for the questionnaire used in this research as well as a rough estimate of the cost of municipal administrative delay. In a different but related field, Thomas Muller and Franklin J. James presented a report at the 1975 annual meeting of the American Real Estate and Urban Economics Association, on housing costs induced by environmental impact review processes.[29] Muller and James argue that environmental review of community land use plans would benefit the environmental impact review (EIR) process, which is currently evolving from an isolated ad hoc procedure into an integral component of the local comprehensive planning process. They estimate the costs of the EIR process to housing developments amount to between 0.4 and 0.7 percent of housing value. Muller and James conclude that the direct costs of environmental review procedures are quite insignificant.

Their figures for the unit cost of the EIR procedure are comparable with those presented in this study. In sum, in examining both the state permit review and its impact on housing costs, this study seeks to provide a clearer understanding of one aspect of the regulatory process, and, in so doing, broaden our understanding of the regulatory process as a whole.

NOTES

1. Commission on Marine Science, Engineering, and Resources, 1969, pp. 2, 49.
2. Ketchum, 1972, p. 103.
3. House of Representatives Report No. 92-1049, p. 11.
4. Commission on Marine Science, Engineering, and Resources, 1969, pp. 73-74.
5. Senate Report No. 92-753, p. 3.
6. Commission on Marine Science, Engineering, and Resources, 1969, pp. 87-88.
7. Senate Report No. 92-753, p. 3.
8. Ketchum, 1972, pp. 103-104.
9. Policy Positions of the National Governor's Conference, 1971, p. 34.
10. Council of State Governments, 1974, p. 34.

11. Hite and Stepp, 1971, preface.
12. Committee on Commerce, Series No. 92-15, p. 252.
13. Sorenson, 1971, p. 3.
14. Hollings, 1973, pp. 115-118.
15. Hite and Stepp, 1971, pp. 20-32.
16. Armstrong, *et al.*, 1974, p. 1, Schnidman and Kendall, 1975, p. 1
17. Armstrong, *et al.*, 1974, p. 1
18. Knecht, 1973, p. 120.
19. Office of Coastal Zone Management, 1974, pp. 1-50.
20. Armstrong, *et al.*, 1974, pp. 5-23.
21. Armstrong, *et al.*, 1974, pp. 24-43; Clark, 1974, pp. 87-110.
22. Sorenson and Demers, 1973; Laird, *et al.*, 1973.
23. Bresson, *et al.*, 1968; Coastal Coordinating Council, 1973.
24. Armstrong, *et al.*, 1974, pp. 152-165.
25. Schwaderer, 1975.
26 Armstrong, *et al.*, 1974, pp. 85-122
27 Armstrong, *et al.*, 1974, p. 86.
28. Bergman, 1975, pp. 527-536.
29. Muller and James, 1975.

Chapter 3

The Origins of Coastal Zone Management

The concept of coastal zone management is not revolutionary but rather evolutionary, an extension and melding of a maturing awareness of environmental sensitivity.

Many of the concepts and procedures currently being employed in coastal zone planning originated with early resource management programs. The basic soil classification and principles of soil behavior developed by the Soil Conservation Service of the Department of Agricultural for specific agricultural uses have been extended to deal with nonrural and urban coastal environments.

The principles for managing soils and controlling water which were developed during the 1930s specifically for runoff control, drainage, irrigation, and water storage provided the foundation for resource management. Siting criteria are being developed directly from soil survey determinations regarding a range of factors: the slope and developmental capacity of steep areas; fluctuating water tables; the load bearing capacity of the soil; the soil's waste product absorption and dissemination capability; the susceptibility of sites to erosion; and the necessity to stabilize soils for continuous development.

Over the years a close working relationship has developed between the Soil Conservation Service and local governments. This cooperation was responsible for the initial introduction of environmental considerations into the land-use regulatory process in the form of individual septic sewer system controls, and more recently, soil disturbance and tree removal permit regulations.

MARINE CONCERNS

Whereas soil and water conservation dominates the ethic in land resource management, coastal zone management has as one of its fundamental goals the maintenance of coastal ecosystems in their optimal condition, which usually means minimizing land-based interference. The ecosystems of coastal zones consist of highly interdependent components and, in an attempt to address these components in their totality, coastal zone resource management has developed the following criteria for classifying components of the coastal ecosystem:

1. *Vital or Preservation Areas:* Ecosystem elements of such critical importance and high value that they are to be preserved intact and protected from disruptive external forces—encompassed within an area of environmental concern.

2. *Environmental Concern or Conservation Areas:* Broad areas of environmetal sensitivity, possibly containing one or more vital areas, the development or use of which must be carefully controlled to protect the ecosystem.

3. *Normal Concern or Utilization Areas:* Regions where only the conservation practices of the land ethic apply to development activities.

Beyond the concepts of ecosystem integrity and interdependence, coastal planning efforts concentrate on water resource management since water provides the essential link between land and sea elements of the coastal ecosystem. The upgrading and monitoring of such water quality variables as basin circulation, runoff, nitrogen content, turbidity, temperature, dissolved oxygen, and salinity are major concerns in coastal zone management. Planning and management activities initially identify those ecologically vital areas which have high storage capacity and productivity, provide abundant and varied habitat, and have a high level of water purity. Some examples of these areas are portrayed in Figure 3. Several crucial related factors are then monitored and attempts are made to control sources of disruption in order to ensure the continued viability of the coastal resource base. The volume, quality, and rate of arrival of fresh water to the coast from both rivers and shoreland watersheds is observed regularly. Floodplains and coastal flood hazard zones are regulated and vegeta-

FIGURE 3

VITAL AREAS IN THE COASTAL ZONE

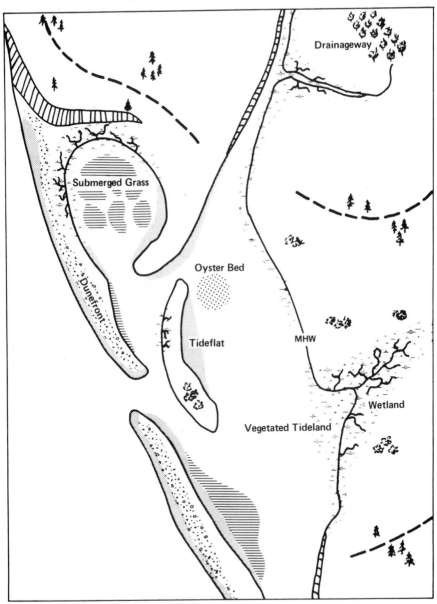

(Clark, 1974, p. 109)

tion buffers are placed at the land-water interface to provide protection and maintain water quality standards.

Regulations are employed to control land and water uses that disrupt critical areas. Adverse impacts are usually identified and controlled via a matrix, as shown in Figure 4, which links particular uses with actual or potential disruption of ambient nutrients, sedimentation. clarity, temperature, dissolved oxygen, salinity, toxicity, and circulation patterns in coastal waters. In addition, land uses in less environmentally sensitive areas are monitored to determine their impact on water quality and are regulated to minimize their adverse impacts on the more critical areas of the coastal ecosystem.

Regulation of cumulative or indirect degradation of the resource base is an extremely complex matter and is, in part, controlled through devices such as density transfers and growth control. Bishop[2] has developed a diagram which illustrates a system for measuring unstable human and natural resources, as shown in Figure 5. The process of analyzing the coastal area's "carrying capacity" involves measuring its ecological or natural resources and identifying the intrinsic constraints these impose upon population density and development. The balance struck between the natural and human components will determine the extent to which the environment will remain productive; too much emphasis on the human or social system runs the risk of exceeding the carrying capacity of the natural system upon which it is based.

Resource management concepts can be seen in many aspects in the control of growth and they have been singularly successful in preempting some of the local land-use powers to higher levels of government through federal and state statutes. Legislative and judicial forays into the designation of environmental resource units and recognition of their significance to the general social welfare have been particularly important in this regard. Randall Scott, in *Management and Control of Growth*, pointed out:

> that localities are not the "logical" jurisdictions for growth limitations (even though they have inherited the power to do so from the state) both for the reasons . . . regarding regional inefficiencies and inequities, and because communities are not necessarily rational, ecological planning units. Nor in some cases do they have the required expertise.[3]

Resource management concepts applied to the coastal zone rein-

FIGURE 4

POTENTIAL FOR ECOSYSTEM DISTURBANCE ASSOCIATED WITH VARIOUS INDUSTRIAL ACTIVITIES

INDUSTRIAL ACTIVITY \ WASTEWATER CHARACTERISTIC	SUSPENDED SOLIDS	DISSOLVED SOLIDS	NITROGEN	PHOSPHORUS	TURBIDITY	TEMPERATURE	DISSOLVED GASSES	COLLOIDAL SOLIDS	pH	COLOR	HEAVY METALS	CYANIDE	VOLATILE ORGANICS	DETERGENTS	FOAMING	PESTICIDES	PHENOL	SULFIDES	OIL AND GREASE	BOD	COD	COLIFORM (FECAL)	COLIFORM (TOTAL)
PAPER AND ALLIED PRODUCTS	○	○	△	△	△	△	○	○	○	○	○		⊙		○				△		△		
GRAIN MILLING AND DAIRY PRODUCTS	○	○	○	○	○	○		○	○	○				○	○				○	○	○	○	△
TEXTILES	○	△	△	○	○	○		○	○	△	△			○	○				○	○	○	○	NA
SEAFOODS AND MEAT PRODUCTS	○	○	○	○	○	○	△		○					○				△	△	○	○	△	NA
PHARMACEUTICALS	△	○	○	○	○	○	△	○	○	○	○	△	○	○					○	○	○		○
LEATHER TANNING AND FINISHING	△	△		△	○		○	○	○	○	○		○	○			△	△	△	△			○
SUGAR, BEVERAGES, FRUITS/VEGETABLES	○	○	△	△	○	○	○		○	○			○	○	○	○				○	○		○
PETROLEUM REFINING		○		△		△	○		○		△	△	○				△	△		△			○
PLASTIC/SYNTHETIC MATERIALS	○	○	△	△	○	○		○	○		○		○	○			○		○	○	○		
BLAST FURNACES, STEEL WORKS[1]	○	○		△	○	△	○	○	○		○	○	○	○			○	○	○				
ORGANIC CHEMICALS	○	○	○	△		○	○		○		△	○	○	○	○		○	○	○	○	○		○
METAL FINISHING	○	△	○	○	○		○		○	○		△	○	○					△				
INORGANIC FERTILIZERS		△		○	NA	○	○		○	NA				NA			NA	NA	NA	○			
ELECTRIC AND STEAM POWER GENERATION		△	△	△		△		○		△	△	○	○	○			△		△				
ALUMINUM	△		△	○	○	○	○		○	○		○		○					△				
FLAT GLASS, CEMENT, LIME[2]		○	△	○	○	○		○	○	○				○									
INORGANIC CHEMICALS		○	△	△	NA	○		NA	○	NA	○	○		NA			NA	NA				NA	NA
INDUSTRIAL GAS PRODUCTS			△	△		○			○					NA					△				

POTENTIAL ECOLOGICAL IMPACT OF INDUSTRIAL WASTEWATER, BY INDUSTRIAL TYPE (SOURCE: U.S. ENVIRONMENTAL PROTECTION AGENCY).

△ – SEVERE   NA – DATA NOT AVAILABLE

○ – VARIABLE   [1] ALSO "ROLLING AND FINISHING"

– SLIGHT   [2] ALSO "CONCRETE PRODUCTS, GYPSUM AND ASBESTOS"

FIGURE 5

THE CARRYING CAPACITY PLANNING PROCESS

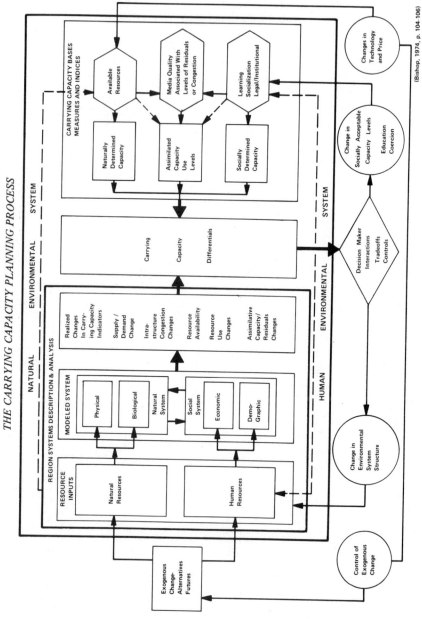

(Bishop, 1974, p. 104-106)

force and probably form the vanguard of the trend in land-use theory toward more involvement by higher levels of government, as it is applied to environmentally sensitive areas. Natural resource management protects environmentally sensitive lands in coastal communities and ensures less traumatic changes in the land that is eventually converted. The concepts of human and natural resource management provide a new dimension in land-use theory by incorporating social and ecological elements into the planning process.

MODIFICATION OF THE TRADITIONAL LAND-USE SYSTEM

Traditionally, a municipality used either its own legal powers or those delegated by the state to establish certain limitations on the use of land within its jurisdiction. These restrictions, in the form of zoning and subdivision controls, were rather inflexible constraints on land use and were frequently obsolete. Procedural inefficiencies or incongruities rather than social or ecological sensitivity were the catalysts for change. The regulations provided a minimal set of standards which, though they prohibited particular misuses of the land, did not actively encourage optimum land use.

The traditional land use system included developing a master plan based upon physical, economic, and demographic data. The plan attempted to project the demand for specific uses, which were accommodated through preset zoning and subdivision controls. Whereas this system had the advantage of being self-administering (i.e. if a development met ordinance requirements, it automatically received approval), the community's land use was often insensitive to conflicting objectives in the public and private sectors.[4]

In contrast to the traditional local land use system, the emerging system reflects an increased awareness of the necessity of sound management of our resources, both natural and social, and a recognition of the need for multilevel government coordination in policy, objectives, and mechanisms affecting land use. Now, given regional assessments of growth, natural constraints, and physical infrastructure limitations (Figure 6), local jurisdictions may establish their land holding capacities by incorporating multiple constraints in their regulatory process. Probably the most basic consideration in the emerging land

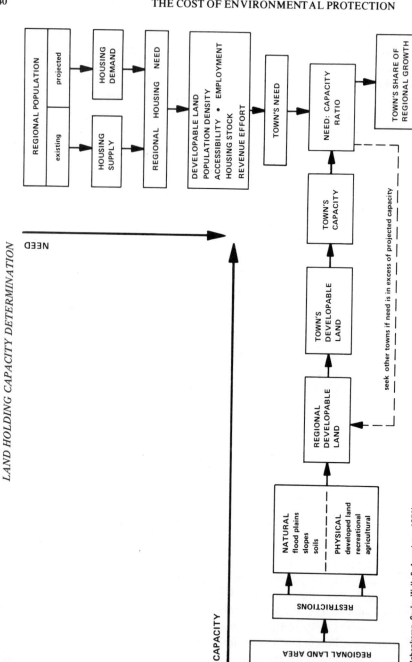

FIGURE 6

LAND HOLDING CAPACITY DETERMINATION

(Rahenkamp, Sachs, Wells & Associates, 1973)

use system is the capacity of natural systems to tolerate development. Recognition of this concern in land-use policy and control may currently be observed in the Duxbury, Massachusetts master plan:

> Future development patterns and the appropriate relationships of various land uses to one another are closely tied to the inherent environmental framework of the town. An understanding of the interrelationships between geology, topography, soils, vegetation, drainage ways, ground water, and development provide a necessary background for constructive land planning. A thorough awareness of the potentials and limitations of the various facets of the Town's natural physical composition is essential as these are primary determinants of land use and development feasibility. Only by respecting the ecology of the town can the natural environmental assets . . . be enhanced and sound development patterns established.[5]

The Duxbury plan provides a practical example of the fact that environmental factors such as slope, vegetation, soil porosity, and permeability when measured individually have limited application in assessing the capacities of natural systems. However, their utility is greatly increased when a constraint is developed which incorporates the indicative aspects of several of these factors. The amount of impervious surface is one such constraint, and it has been established in some of the more innovative regulatory ordinances.[6] With the establishment of impervious cover limits for each tract of land in a community, the environment can be protected by utilizing natural drainage systems.[7] This offers a tangible advantage over artificial drainage systems, which tend to produce erosion and subsequent sediment pollution in waterways, wetlands, and marshes. The destructive impact of altering natural drainage was recognized by the Duxbury Planning Board:

> Activities which degrade water quality, reduce the water storage capacity of the land, or interfere with the natural flow patterns of the water courses should be prohibited.[8]

A community's land holding capacity is also determined by its existing infrastructure. Road, water, and sewerage systems place definite constraints upon the conversion of land and upon its ultimate capacity. The worst effects of urban sprawl have underscored the limited ability of municipalities to absorb new land uses and the need for their land-use systems to guide development where it can best be served by public facilities.[9] Any new development must be evaluated against the inherent physical capacity of a community's local or regional infrastructure.

Plans must account not only for community capacity to absorb development, but also for the amount and type of development pressure to be expected in the future. Traditional techniques have measured this pressure through the projection of historical trends in population growth, but more recent techniques incorporate a number of additional factors. These population growth estimates, along with an inventory of regional housing supply, are used to provide an assessment of housing need for a particular future year, commonly a twenty-year projection. Instead of allocating housing units that will be required in the future to individual municipalities on the basis of prior growth and available, uncommitted land, allocation of housing units is based upon additional factors such as natural capacity of the land, existing population density, highway access, employment concentration, housing stock, and revenue base. More housing units are then allocated to communities better able to accommodate increased population. Communities in which population density is already high, the network of highways is limited, employment opportunities are sparse, housing is already overburdened, or taxation is excessively heavy are allocated fewer housing units.

A final element in the review of new development is consideration of the relationship between cost of the development and incoming revenues in the community. A town's financial situation is highly dependent upon land use. The land uses permitted under the impervious surface constraint serve to illustrate, in Figure 7, the variability of the cost-revenue balance.[10] A mixture of densities is necessary in order to maintain the solvency of local governments over the long term; creative, more intensive site design provides a good means of accommodating growth without endangering the fiscal balance in a community.

Innovative master plans have incorporated these considerations to more clearly define a community's expected share of growth and delineate the constraints acting upon that growth. As a result, the community's environmental, infrastructure, and fiscal limitations on growth are examined in terms directly applicable to the evaluation of a proposed development. Implementation of such master plans seems to require a more flexible set of land-use regulations than was the case in

FIGURE 7

FISCAL IMPACT OF LAND USE AS AFFECTED BY
ENVIRONMENTAL CONSTRAINTS

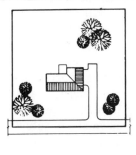

SINGLE FAMILY
COVERAGE   16%
DENSITY   1 DU/AC
VALUE $ 50,000.00
or $ 45,000.00

TAX YIELD $2200.00
MUNICIPAL COST   2052.00
SURPLUS $ 148.00
                 [$ 72.00]

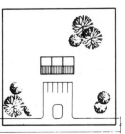

TOWNHOUSE
COVERAGE   16%
DENSITY   3 DU/AC
VALUE $105,000.00

TAX YIELD $4620.00
MUNICIPAL COST   4216.00
SURPLUS $ 404.00

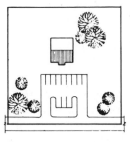

GARDEN APARTMENT
COVERAGE   16%
DENSITY   6 DU/AC
VALUE $150,000.00

TAX YIELD $6600.00
MUNICIPAL COST   5084.00
SURPLUS $1516.00

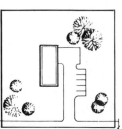

INDUSTRIAL
COVERAGE   16%
VALUE $50,000.00

TAX YIELD $2200.00
MUNICIPAL COST   910.00
SURPLUS $1290.00

the past. Flexibility implies a blend of rigid zoning for critical areas and more broadly defined controls for developable land. Development outside rigid zones proceeds according to a rather flexible process of negotiation between the town and the developer. (Figure 8). The administration of this process, however, must take place according to the constraints outlined in the master plan.

Another modification in traditional land use control is the shift from local to state, regional, and national planning programs. In the coastal zone management program, supervisory authority is vested in the state. Major facility sitings are handled through a permitting or licensing mechanism at the state level and incremental commitments of land to development are monitored by the state to control the cumulative impact on environmental, social, and fiscal systems. Ideally, in implementing the coastal zone managment program, local authorities would have the power to control land use within their own jurisdictions according to the guidelines established by a state policy.

The setting aside of environmentally or culturally critical areas and the emphasis on water as a link and indicator of adverse impact reflect the influence of resource management on traditional land use planning. Examples of this influence may be found in Duxbury, Mass., the Lake Tahoe region, Sparta and Ramapo, N.J., and to some extent, Medford, N.J.

REGULATORY MECHANISMS REFLECTING A POLICY OF RESOURCE MANAGEMENT

Coastal zone planning and resource management require a comprehensive understanding of problems affecting the entire shoreland region. Such a perspective is often out of reach for municipalities. Consequently, there has been a growing realization that the traditional methods—dealing with particular issues and fragments of environmental systems—have frequently been counter-productive. National and state legislative efforts to focus attention on the state as the agent of land management are attempts to establish a more comprehensive planning and resource management approach.[11] Under such an approach management authority may be delegated to various levels of government within the state according to the concept that land-use decision making may occur at the lowest level of government consistent with

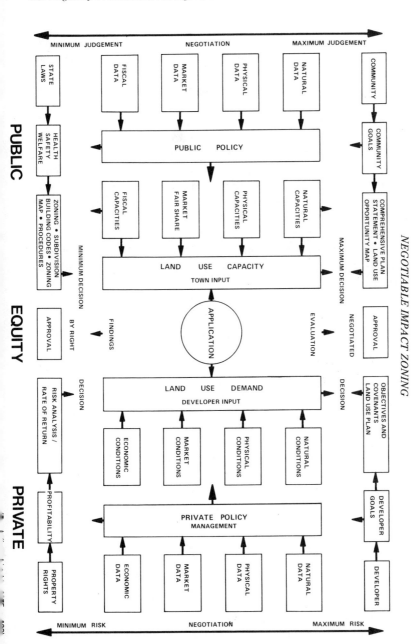

FIGURE 8

NEGOTIABLE IMPACT ZONING

the scope of an activity. The lower level government decisions would, of course, have to be consistent with the goals and restrictions articulated by successively higher levels.[12] In practice, decision making at the lowest level would concern activities which would have a relatively limited impact, whereas decisions involving more extensive impact would be referred to a higher authority.

Coastal states engaging in management programs seem to be concentrating their energies on a limited number of development decisions in order to avoid excessive use of the police power. State permitting of major facilities, as noted in an earlier chapter, has become a rather integral, if not primary, component of the coastal zone management program in many states. Along with shoreline zoning, it has given the state direct control over major land-use activities and critical areas in the coastal zone. Regulation through permit procedures is commonly instituted by federal and state statutes which preempt local police powers, particularly in the realm of resource management.

The permit procedure has been utilized as a regulatory device for a considerable period of time. The issuance of permits may be classified in three general categories. First, in the ad hoc, permit-by-permit approach, no explicit criteria are issued, and the regulatory program defines a policy only by inference from the record of approvals and denials. The process is incremental; there is no guarantee of consistency. A second type of permit system enforces a restrictive order such as that pertaining to a critical area (e.g., wetlands). The order mandates what can and cannot be done to change restricted areas. A third type of permit system is carried out in conformance with a general management scheme; this last system is the most effective method to determine the acceptability of a proposed activity. The system of state permitting of major facilities in the coastal zone may conceivably take any one of the three general forms. However, its widespread use as an interim control device has largely reflected the first or *ad hoc* approach.

Viable state coastal zone management programs, founded in land-use system and resource management concepts, are dependent upon both reasonable exercise of state police power and a more restricted delegation of state authority to lower levels of government. Major facilities permitting at the state level must be integrated into the local land-use regulatory system, to alleviate the problems that have arisen when municipalities refuse to relinquish land-use prerogatives. As Bosselman and Callies have noted:

> A common failing of most of the new state land regulatory systems is that they do not relate in a logical manner to the continuing need for local participation. Most of them tend to by-pass the existing system of local regulation and set up completely independent and unrelated systems. This requires the developer (and ultimately the consumer) who is subject to both systems to go through two separate and distinct administrative processes, often doubling the time required and substantially increasing the costs required to obtain approval of the development proposal.[13]

NOTES

1. Clark, 1974, introduction.
2. Bishop, 1974, pp. 104-106.
3. Scott, 1975, p. 17
4. Sorenson, 1971, pp. 5-10; Scott, 1975a, pp. 179-296.
5. Duxbury master plan, 1973, p.7.
6. Odell, 1975, p. 25.
7. Wells, 1974, pp. 21-26.
8. Duxbury master plan, 1973, p. 10.
9. Real Estate Research Corporation, 1974, pp. 7-26.
10. Wells, 1974, p. 26.
11. Senate Report No. 92-753, pp. 5-6; Owen, 1970, pp. 59-64.
12. Ketchum, 1972, p. 21.
13. Bosselman and Callies, 1971, p. 320.

Chapter 4

Methodology

SCOPE OF STUDY—BASIC DEFINITIONS

Twenty-one coastal developments in Dover Township which applied for New Jersey's coastal development permit under the Coastal Area Facility Review Act (CAFRA) of 1973 (N.J.S.A. 13:19-1) were inventoried during the spring of 1975. The inventory included all CAFRA applications from this township over the 1973 to 1975 period, totaling 32 percent of all New Jersey CAFRA applications. The costs of meeting each of the land-use regulations in effect for the Dover Township, New Jersey area and the steps involved in the subdivision process were identified for each project. The cost-data sets were established through a series of interviews with residential developers, engineers, architectural and planning consultants, attorneys, and governmental officials involved with developments in the area.

For purposes of this study, the land conversion process is limited to the subdivision stage or land acquisition/platting/permitting/bonding/approved land sale sequence which occurs prior to physical site preparation. Sample developments were investigated from the time that land was acquired, through the stages of local, county, and state regulatory approval and, finally, to the point of passing the land on to the builder. The land remains in its original state throughout the processing phase; upon final plat approval, the tract becomes a conglomerate of subdivided, municipally approved, yet physically unimproved, lots.

Residential developers are defined here as land developers, speculators, or realtors, and comprise private individuals, groups, or corporate bodies which directly sponsor a project. The residential developer acquires the land either through simple purchase, land lease, or option. He obtains all the approvals and transfers the project to a contractor who will erect the structure and market the development. This definition excludes private entrepreneurs or corporate bodies engaged in actual alteration of the land after the subdivision or regulatory phase has been completed. It should be made clear, however, that the residential developer can be, and frequently is, involved in both converting and developing land; the term "packaging" or passing on an approved parcel of land may apply to only a portion of the developments within the sample—obviously some owners may prefer to retain the approved land and improve it themselves.

SELECTION OF STUDY AREA

In selecting the study area, several considerations were foremost. In order to assess both the administrative and financial impact of state review of major facilities in coastal zones, it was felt that the study area should exhibit considerable development activity within a regulated coastal area. Beyond this, the area selected for investigation had to be contained within a single local political jurisdiction to minimize the influence of conflicting local land-use policies. Since the research was to be done in the New Jersey coastal zone, it was also necessary for the area to be outside the regulation of the New Jersey Wetlands Act (N.J.S.A. 13:9A-1) because the research design required land with viable development rights in order to assess the response of the free market system to coastal land-use regulation.

This combination of factors suggested portions of Ocean County, New Jersey (Figure 9) as a plausible research site. Located in the center of New Jersey's Atlantic coastal zone, the county is literally an interface between the development pressures of urban North Jersey, including the New York metropolitan region, and the environmental fragility of rural South Jersey, including the Pine Forests. The county, part of the outer ring of the New York metropolitan region, is currently the site of massive single-family and multifamily residential growth and is one of the few remaining areas offering reasonably priced new housing within the New York region. There is some evidence indicating additional population pressures from the Delaware Valley region, via the Atlantic City Expressway, but these stimuli are subordinate to those emanating from New York. The county's location between two ex-

FIGURE 9

OCEAN COUNTY, NEW JERSEY

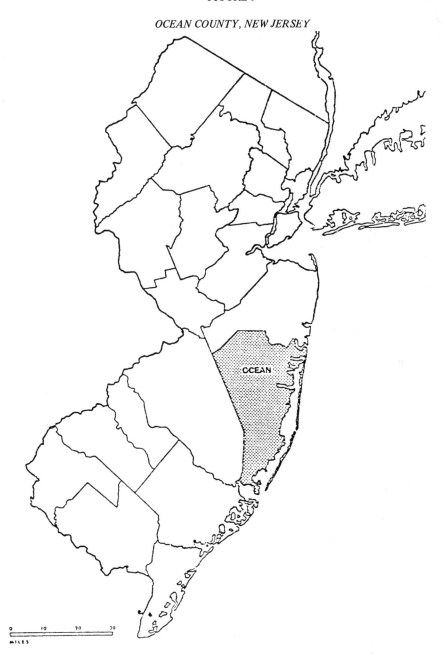

panding urban nodes, New York and Philadelphia, and its proximity to the Jersey shore, an extensively used recreational area, create severe development pressures, potentially more intense than any other coastal county in the state.

Several statistics confirm these points. Ocean County's average decennial growth rate from 1950 to 1970 was in excess of 90 percent; a substantially greater rate than that exhibited by other central Jersey counties over the previous twenty years (Figure 10). Whereas in the last decade, growth in every other central county declined, the population base of Ocean County continued to expand, nearly doubling from 1960 to 1970.[1] The county's age distribution remained relatively constant, despite population gains, with slight shifts from preschool and mature working-age classes to school and retirement age categories. This is a function of the development of modestly priced housing which attracts families with school-age children and planned retirement communities attracting the elderly. The natural population increase stands at 0.5 percent annually, with inmigration about four times that rate. Of the counties constituting the outer ring of the metropolitan New York region, Ocean County is the primary source of new housing and the only one to gain more than 100,000 people in the last decade.[2]

The economy of Ocean County, traditionally based upon marine-oriented markets, is now equally composed of service and trade industries with slight impacts from manufacturing and mining. Ocean County's total employment is forecast to increase 63.7 percent from 1970 to 1980 as the result of a transition from a tourist to a year-round economy. Employment figures indicate at least 21,000 residents commute to jobs outside the county, indicating Ocean County is a labor export region within the state.[3] While the distribution of income for county workers mirrors the state distribution, the county's median family income of $9,246 is about 18 percent lower than the state's $11,407. This again reflects the county's appeal for those desiring low- to moderate-income housing near the New York metropolitan area.

For the ten years preceding the current economic slump, annual housing starts grew at a rate of approximately 8 percent. Since 1962, nearly 110,000 new building lots have been created through the subdivision of 35,000 acres, constituting 8.5 percent of the total land area of the county.[4] During the same period, slightly over 42,000 building permits were issued throughout the county.[5] These statistics indicate

FIGURE 10

COMPARATIVE COUNTY POPULATION GROWTH RATES

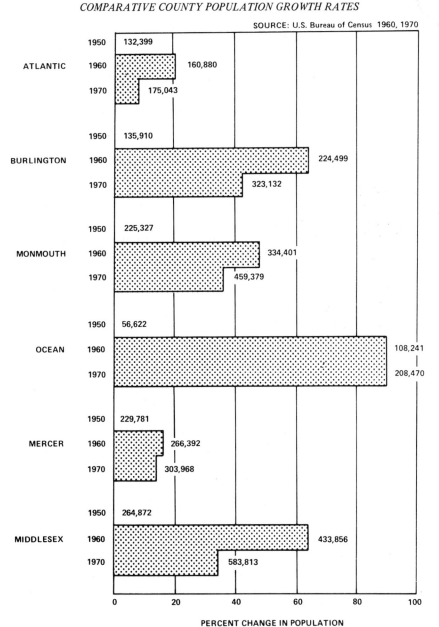

SOURCE: U.S. Bureau of Census 1960, 1970

PERCENT CHANGE IN POPULATION

that approximately 38 percent of the subdivided lots were actually developed, compared to the national average of 17 percent of all new lots actually, being developed.[6] Obviously, New Jersey's coastal counties are already under significant development pressure, and the pressure is bound to increase. As of 1973, 40 percent, or 162,325 acres, of the land within Ocean County exclusive of wetlands and flood plains remained undeveloped or in agricultural uses. A comparison of land availability and county population and economic pressure forecasts indicates significant residential and nonresidential development in Ocean County over the next several decades.

The statewide distribution of Coastal Area Facility Review Act (CAFRA) applications provides an indication of the intensity of development activity in Ocean County compared with other coastal counties in New Jersey. As shown in Table 9, of the 121 CAFRA applications made to the state during the first twenty-two months of the act's implementation, almost half were from Ocean County. The frequency of CAFRA applications was used as one indicator to select a township within the county which would meet the second research objective, confinement to one political jurisdiction. As shown in Table 10, Dover Township, New Jersey generated the greatest number of CAFRA permit applications of any municipality in the state. The fact that nearly all of the township is included within the New Jersey CAFRA jurisdiction was another factor which influenced the selection of Dover Township. (The location of Dover Township is shown in Figure 11.)

DEVELOPMENTS SELECTED FOR STUDY

The Dover Township developments which were considered under the Coastal Area Facility Review Act during the first nineteen months of the act's implementation, September 1973 through April 1975, constituted the cases examined in this study. Twenty-three of the township's thirty-one applications during this period were residential[7]—twelve single-family and eleven multifamily developments.

The residential developments in the Dover sample are, by CAFRA's definition, major subdivisions of at least twenty-five dwelling units. The sample, which represents 87 percent of the CAFRA filings within one municipality, is an accurate representation of typical costs and procedures associated with state-regulated residential development.

TABLE 9

DISTRIBUTION OF CAFRA PERMITS IN STATE OF NEW JERSEY
(September 1973 – August 1975)

County	Residential	Sewerage	Industrial	Miscellaneous
Atlantic	10	4	2	1
Cape May	20	1	0	2
Cumberland	1	1	1	0
Middlesex	1	0	0	0
Monmouth	8	6	1	0
Ocean	40	18	2	0
Salem	0	0	0	1
Total	80	31	6	4

Source: Coastal Area Permits Section, Division of Marine Services, Department of Environmental Protection, State of New Jersey.

TABLE 10

DISTRIBUTION OF CAFRA PERMITS AMONG OCEAN COUNTY TOWNSHIPS
(September 1973 — August 1975)

Township	Residential	Sewerage	Industrial	Miscellaneous
Berkeley (Beachwood)	0	1	0	0
Brick (Mantolokin)				
(Pt. Pleasant)	3	4	0	0
Dover	25	8	2	0
Eagleswood	0	0	0	0
Lacy	0	1	0	0
Lakewood	1	0	0	0
Little Egg Harbor	3	0	0	0
Long Beach (Beach Haven)				
(Barnegat) (Harvey Cedars)	2	3	0	0
Manchester	1	1	0	0
Ocean	0	0	0	0
Stafford	0	0	0	0
Union	5	0	0	0
Total	40	18	2	0

Source: Coastal Area Permits Section, Division of Marine Services, Department of Environmental Protection, State of New Jersey.

FIGURE 11

DOVER TOWNSHIP, OCEAN COUNTY, NEW JERSEY

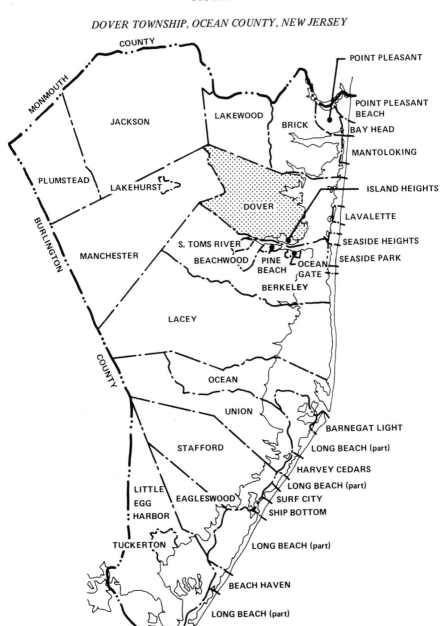

The Dover Township sample is classified according to single-family and multifamily residential use. This classification is necessary since the two types of housing are regulated by somewhat different controls. Of the twelve single-family subdivisions applying for CAFRA permits, eleven were inventoried; of eleven multifamily developments, nine were successfully examined.

It should be noted that the properties included as cases in the survey may not all have been developed. An assessment of the regulatory process as it applies to predevelopment activities constitutes the scope of this analysis.

INTERVIEW PROCEDURES

Most residential developers and consulting firms involved in land conversion in New Jersey are small in scale, with owners themselves performing most of the functions in the purchase and development process. It was felt, therefore, that the most productive contact with these individuals would be a personal interview. Seventy-nine interviews were conducted with developers, consulting engineers, architects, traffic consultants, attorneys, township officials, county officials, state officials, and federal officials.

The majority of the developers contacted in the field survey were identified through the CAFRA files at the Department of Environmental Protection, Trenton, New Jersey. Additional participants were identified by developers during the first series of interviews. Persons responsible for regulating land subdivision or CAFRA processing in state, county, and local government, were identified by department heads.

Cost and processing-time data for the projects were obtained directly from tallies of expenses and surveys of municipal records pertaining to the proposed projects. A variety of bookkeeping procedures had to be taken into account; in several cases a succession of principals were involved, and multiple plan submittals were commonplace. Information obtained from the residential developers regarding mortgages, taxes, sale prices, and status of title were checked where possible via public records.

The interviews with governmental officials were especially helpful in fulfilling three of the research objectives. First, state and local officials provided the background information and materials necessary to design the survey used to secure information. Second, in instances in which a few of the proposed projects were still in the early stages of the regulatory procedure, township and county officials provided invaluable assistance in estimating applicable governmental fees for the project's final stages. Finally, township officials provided current information as to administrative procedures, departmental responsibility, and local interpretation of coastal land-use regulations.

THE SURVEY

The survey was patterned after the questionnaire for developers used in the Rutgers University Center for Urban Policy Research publication, *Zoning and Housing Costs*.[8] As a result of recent research,[9] a revised version of the Rutgers questionnaire was developed for this study (Appendix A). The questionnaire was then pretested for two developments. From these examples, additional information was gained concerning the enormous number and levels of regulations affecting residential development in the coastal zone and the critical nature of processing time. As a result, the questionnaire was redesigned to incorporate all possible combinations and levels of government approvals necessary for development.

The questionnaire is divided into four major sections. The first section covers the purchase date of the tract, the buyer and seller, the acreage, the price per acre, and the zoning classification. This information is used to determine the time at which the subdivision process began and the form of ownership of the site. Peculiar land assignment transactions and the specifics of assignment options were also covered in the first section, as well as information pertaining to necessary, but ancillary, zoning appeals. The second portion of the questionnaire dealt with information regarding the type of development being proposed and its history. This section also solicited an actual or estimated sales price for the land, assuming all approvals had been granted. Specific processing time and costs associated with the subdivision process were covered in the third portion of the questionnaire. A data matrix was designed to include all levels of governmental land-use controls and related regulations such as those imposed by municipal, utility, or environmental agencies. Information regarding time intervals, consulting costs, and governmental fees encountered at each stage of subdivision processing was also solicited. The developer's carrying costs, examined in the last section of the questionnaire, were the most difficult data to obtain and verify. All figures were derived from interviews with the source of the expense, and cross checked with both the developer and government records. Property taxes, interest charges, invested equity, mortgage outstanding, and foregone opportunity costs constituted the costs carried by the residential developer during the regulatory phase of the project.

ANALYTICAL AND GRAPHICAL PROCEDURES

The analytical and statistical procedures used in this study are descriptive. Time periods for processing associated with various stages of regulatory approval are derived from modal times experienced by the sample projects. Processing times for individual regulations cover the period from submission of an application to approval of the application. Data was also compiled to detail the expenses incurred by the residential developer when complying with both local and state land-use controls. A cost matrix of coastal zone land use regulations is reproduced as Appendix B. The dwelling unit cost of each of the items of subdivision processing was determined by adding the costs for consulting, legal, and government regulatory fees and apportioning this total among the number of units in the proposed development. The costs associated with CAFRA permitting were obtained for each project and expressed on a per unit base. Engineering and legal fees could not always be broken down to charges for each regulation. In the few instances in which this was not possible, the average distribution for the other cases was used. Table 11 shows the distribution employed for both single-family and multifamily cases. Legal fees, when not specifically detailed, were assigned on a 75-25 percent basis to preliminary and final platting (in the single-family case) or on a 50-50 percentage basis to site plan review and zoning variance procedures (in the multifamily case).

A graphical timeline—calibrated in months and covering the duration of the regulatory process for each project—was used to calculate the cost of subdivision processing. Regulatory costs were entered into the graph at the particular time of their occurrence in the process, (that is, as each plat, site plan, or permit application was required). Subdivision costs included the cost of the initial land acquisition, mortgage, interest, taxes, and carrying costs. The cost of land acquisi-

TABLE 11

DISTRIBUTION OF ENGINEERING AND CONSULTING FEES
FOR LOCAL APPROVALS

Single-Family Case		Multifamily Case	
Item	*Factor*	*Item*	*Factor*
Sketch Plat	.209	Sketch Site Plan	.204
Preliminary Plat	.282	Site Plan Review	.619
Final Plat	.312	Zoning Variance	.012
Preliminary Sewer	.015	Preliminary Sewer	.015
Tentative Sewer	.012	Tentative Sewer	.012
Final Sewer	.029	Final Sewer	.029
Fire Comm. Review	.026	Fire Comm. Review	.026
Soil Disturb. Permit	.031	Soil Disturb. Permit	.031
Tree Removal Permit	.033	Tree Removal Permit	.033
Wetlands Permit	.031	County Reviews	.014
Shade Tree Bond Prep.	.006		
County Reviews	.014		
Total	1.000	Total	1.000

Assumptions:

1. Wetlands when not applicable is applied to preliminary plat.
2. Shade tree bond when not applicable is applied to preliminary plat.
3. Site plan combines preliminary and final plat.
4. Zoning figures are actual quotation or .012 adjustment factor.
5. Surety bonds are based upon fees of $15.00 per thousand.

tion was frequently found in the form of an initial down payment for the first month and monthly mortgage and interest payments for the duration of the processing of the development. Taxes were entered in the timeline on a quarterly basis. All expenses incurred during the period of compliance with coastal land-use regulations were carried for the remaining months of the process at a foregone opportunity cost of 15 percent annually.[10]

Given various regulatory policies, the cost of the subdivision process may be determined through a series of monthly calculations beginning with the first month of the process and utilizing the formula:

$$[(L+I+T)+R+Cm_1] K = C$$ Carrying costs for a particular month)

$$[(L+I+T)+R+C] = M$$ (Total expenses for the month)

$$Cm_1 + M = Cm_2$$ (Cumulative costs of project to date)

The signs in the formula may be explained as follows:

L represents land cost in that month, I is interest in that month, T is taxes in that month, R equals the regulatory cost of obtaining project approvals during that month, Cm_1 represents the cumulative expenses of all preceding months, K is a constant factor of 0.0125 reflecting a straight 15 percent annual rate by month, C is the carrying costs for the month, M represents the total expense incurred by the developer in that month, and Cm_2 equals the cumulative cost of the project including the cost of current month. Calculations must be repeated for each successive month in the subdivision process beginning with the first month.

NOTES

1. Ocean County Planning Board, 1972, p. 4.
2. Ocean County Planning Board, 1972, pp. 16-18, 26.
3. Oross, 1974a, pp. 20, 24.
4. Oross, 1973, p. 13.
5. Sagalyn and Sternlieb, 1973, p. 101.
6. Reilly, 1973, p. 264.

7. Commercial and sewer applications have been excluded from this analysis.
8. Sagalyn and Sternlieb, 1973, pp. 116-124.
9. Real Estate Research Corporation, 1974; Nieswand, Stillman, and Esser, 1973; Kenney, 1972, pp. 237-245; Daugherty, 1974, pp. 30-32.
10. The 15 percent annual rate for carrying costs, used throughout this analysis, is a relatively conservative figure in contrast to the 20 percent annual rate suggested by Lindeman, 1974, p. 46.

Chapter 5

Standard Development Process In The Coastal Zone

LAND CONVERSION

State coastal zone management programs impose prohibitions on many commercial and industrial uses in coastal areas as well as on all private uses in specified critical locations. Beyond these outright moratoriums, coastal states have also opted for permit procedures to control the conversion of coastal land for residential uses. New Jersey, along with most coastal states, considers the incremental conversion of coastal land to residential development to be the most acute problem in its coastal zone.[2] Unlike the State of Washington[3] but like California,[4] New Jersey is implementing a program to grant major facilities permits prior to the formulation of a coastal management program. The state's use of major facilities permits has not resulted in a moratorium on all development within the coastal zone. A developer whose site design reflects environmental sensitivity, as detailed by guidelines formulated by the state, is granted approval to proceed with his development. Although the state permit may not authorize the development as originally conceived by either the developer or municipality and processing costs may increase, development activities authorized by the state continue, albeit at a slower pace.[5]

The continual flow of residents and commercial activities into coastal areas indicates that the zone will face increasing pressure for development, even under the most stringent land-use regulations. According to the Rockefeller Task Force on Land Use and Urban Growth, the interaction of intensive development pressures and stringent regulation provides the best opportunity for the creation of a more sensitive land conversion process. The synthesis of these conflicting forces may only come about within an economically viable housing market, in which the effects of control are plainly visible. An improvement in the quality and quantity of market information available to the developer, via a predictable and integrated state-local coastal regulatory system, is an essential first step in upgrading the efficiency and quality of land conversion. Once this system has evolved, there is a distinct potential for earlier processing, lower costs to the developer, and eventually reduced costs to the housing consumer.

The remaining chapters of this study assess the impact of state permit procedures on the local subdivision process. Taking a single municipality as an example, the development and subdivision processes are typified for New Jersey's coastal zone. The integration of the state's CAFRA permit into the standard process will be documented and the subtle inter-relationships of various state administrative policies will be discussed in terms of administrative procedure and processing time. As local subdivision procedure is a derivative of the Standard Planning Enabling Act (1928), officially adopted by most states and passed to their inclusive jurisdictions, New Jersey's experience has national applicability.

THE RESIDENTIAL DEVELOPMENT PROCESS

There are four basic components involved in the decision-making process for residential developments, as shown in Figure 12. The process of residential development in the coastal zone is essentially the same as that for other areas in which land conversion occurs. The process begins with a residential developer who desires to convert coastal land. The method of land acquisition may be in the form of a single tract or a complex series of parcel assemblages. The process of acquiring land requires the assistance of several specialists, agents, and lenders. Market analysts and appraisers aid the developer in selecting suitable areas for residential developments; real estate brokers handle the actual sale of the land. Frequently the developer has to borrow money through a loan agent such as a mortgage broker or a mortgage correspondent. Other specialized personnel involved during the land acquisition phase may include a title attorney, accountant, or market researcher.

The second phase of the development process involves subdivision of the land into smaller sites or plots subject to the local re-

FIGURE 12

RESIDENTIAL LAND DEVELOPMENT DECISION SYSTEM MODEL

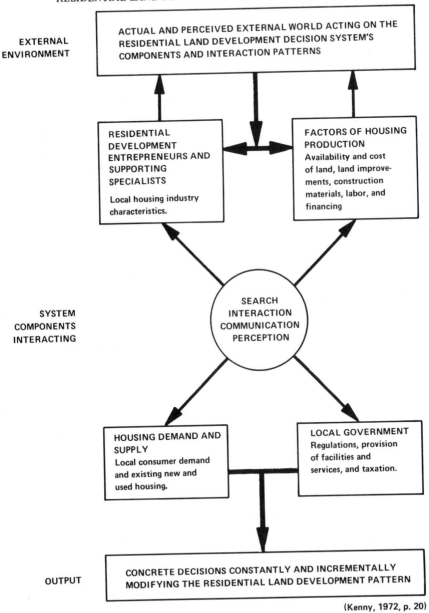

EXTERNAL
ENVIRONMENT

ACTUAL AND PERCEIVED EXTERNAL WORLD ACTING ON THE
RESIDENTIAL LAND DEVELOPMENT DECISION SYSTEM'S
COMPONENTS AND INTERACTION PATTERNS

RESIDENTIAL
DEVELOPMENT
ENTREPRENEURS AND
SUPPORTING
SPECIALISTS

Local housing industry
characteristics.

FACTORS OF HOUSING
PRODUCTION
Availability and cost
of land, land improve-
ments, construction
materials, labor, and
financing

SYSTEM
COMPONENTS
INTERACTING

SEARCH
INTERACTION
COMMUNICATION
PERCEPTION

HOUSING DEMAND AND
SUPPLY
Local consumer demand
and existing new and
used housing.

LOCAL GOVERNMENT
Regulations, provision
of facilities and
services, and taxation.

OUTPUT

CONCRETE DECISIONS CONSTANTLY AND INCREMENTALLY
MODIFYING THE RESIDENTIAL LAND DEVELOPMENT PATTERN

(Kenny, 1972, p. 20)

gulatory system. In this phase, the residential developer incurs the expense of land survey, placement of plot boundary markers, environmental permit applications, utility reviews, and submittal of the surveyor's plat of the proposed subdivision for official approval. An architect, engineer, environmentalist, attorney, planner, and governmental representative commonly aid the residential developer through this phase of the project. It should be noted that the process of subdividing does not require any physical change in the landscape. The paper subdivision merely gives notice of intent to convert the raw land into an improved site. Once the plat is approved and signed by the duly constituted municipal authorities, bonds are posted and the plat is entered in public records.

Land improvements are carried out in the next development phase with the aid of a general contractor, engineer, surveyor, various municipal inspectors, and public utility representatives. The availability of public utilities significantly affects the cost of site improvement. In general, improvement costs are a function of topography, soil conditions, design layout, and local subdivision policy and quality of supervision. Developments in the coastal zone typically require extensive site preparation in areas which exhibit either poor drainage characteristics or unusual environmental sensitivity.

Housing construction may be phased with or subsequent to site improvement. The residential developer solicits a general contractor who in turn allocates work among multiple subcontractors such as carpenters, plumbers, electricians, plasterers, masons, and as many other tradesmen as are necessary to complete the project. The construction proceeds with periodic inspections by the lender, developer, architect, and government authorities.

It must be emphasized that this is a brief overview of the development process; the procedure can vary significantly. A residential developer can enter or bail out at any point; the land may never be developed beyond the subdivision or site improvement phases. There are innumerable variations in both the process itself and the number and type of agents involved in the process.

THE SUBDIVISION PROCESS

The implementation of state zoning and permitting procedures as envisioned in the coastal zone management program primarily influence the project planning stage of the development process. However, as the Department of Environmental Protection notes in its coastal zone management development grant application:

> Land use control is primarily a local responsibility in New Jersey. Other state agencies do impact on local land use, e.g., Department of Transportation highway construction, but they have no legislated authority for land use control. . . . The only state agency currently authorized to control [general] land use in the coastal zone is the Department of Environmental Protection through its marine law enforcement function which includes riparian right, wetland, and coastal area facility permitting.[7]

In practice, land use regulation administered at the local level has proven less than adequate; the master plan is not steadfastly observed or even kept up to date and rarely, if ever, is the environmental interdependence of communities considered. There has been a consistent pattern of critical land use decisions being reached piecemeal through variance and rezoning procedures. Justified by individual hardship or special circumstance, zoning by exception rather than by rule is a frequent local occurrence.

One of the primary functions of the planning board is to review subdivision and site plan applications following guidelines set forth in the regulations passed by the township committee. The state enabling legislation (N.J.S.A. 40:55-1.2) defines the process of subdivision as follows:

> Subdivision means the division of a lot, tract or parcel of land into 2 or more lots, sites or other divisions of land for the purpose, whether immediate or future, of sale or building development . . . subdivision also includes resubdivision, and where appropriate to the context, relates to the process of subdividing or to the land or territory divided.

Whereas the general framework for subdivision control in New Jersey is provided through this state enabling legislation, individual municipalities implement the specific procedures to be followed. In practice the state enabling statutes introduce a considerable degree of uniformity among the municipal ordinances.

The diagrams of the subdivision process shown in Figures 13 and 14 display the step-by-step procedure for consideration of both single-family and multifamily applications. The municipality originates local

FIGURE 13

SUBDIVISION PROCESS: THE SINGLE-FAMILY CASE

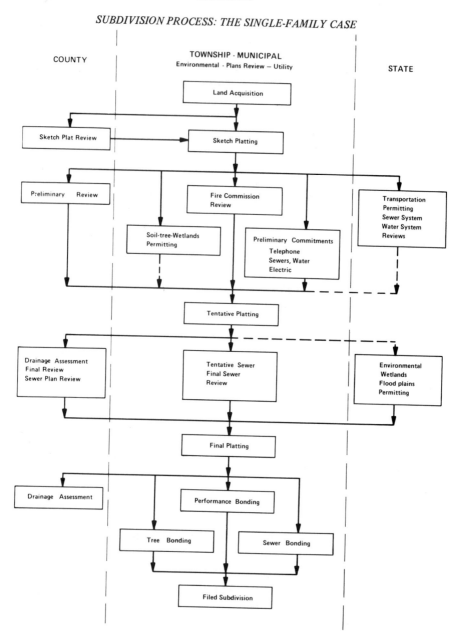

FIGURE 14

SITE PLAN PROCESS: THE MULTIFAMILY CASE

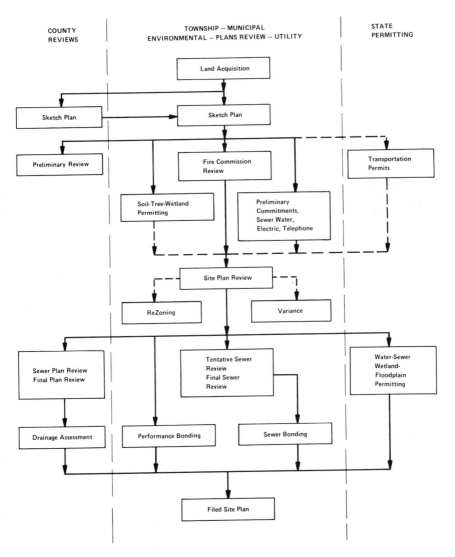

environmental, plan, and utility review procedures and coordinates document referrals to county and state governments. The process of requiring subdivision approval is essentially a five (multifamily) or six (single-family) step procedure. Those steps linked in the diagram by solid lines must be completed before proceeding to the next step. Those connected by broken lines do not require prior approval to move to the next step; however, they must be resolved within two successive steps.

Governmental bodies engaged in land-use decisions, as shown in Figure 15, are as intricately interrelated as the process itself. Figure 15 portrays the allocation of reviews among the various agencies responsible for residential land-use regulation. Where proposed developments require rezoning, the township committee reviews the application; where variance procedures are required, the board of adjustment and the planning board review the application. The township committee is the final link in the sequence, reviewing all matters of rezoning, variances, and bonding. The county has a substantial review capacity and some regulatory authority where projects affect drainage and roadways. The requirement that plats must be filed with the county recording office holds the potential for expansion of county involvement in the regulatory process; however, this mechanism is not currently being pursued.[8] The responsibilities of the state agencies parallel those of the county except in terms of environmental regulation. For residential subdivisions greater than fifty units, state agencies regulate water supply and sewerage; for all subdivisions, the state regulates floodplains, wetlands, and riparian land. Coordination is provided by the local planning board, which plays a central role in land conversion.

The pattern of interaction among governmental regulatory agencies is extremely complex, if not unpredictable. As the coastal zone management program portends increased state control, the potential disruption of the present type and form of agency interaction must be considered a definite possibility. For this reason an examination of the standard subdivision process, prior to state intervention, is vital to this study.

COMPONENTS OF THE SUBDIVISION PROCESS

The standard local platting procedure has been well documented.[9] However, examination of the associated, yet tangential environmental,

FIGURE 15

GOVERNMENT AGENCIES INVOLVED IN THE SUBDIVISION PROCESS

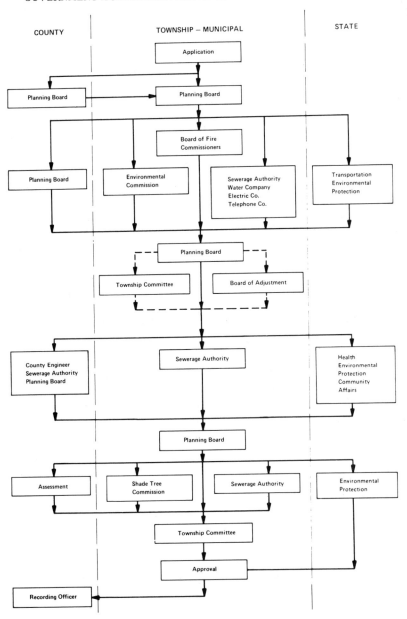

utility, and state approvals have been limited to brief acknowledgments of their existence. The discussion which follows will inject analyses of these associated approvals as well as supplement the traditional rhetoric regarding the platting procedure.

The Sketch Plat

During or after land acquisition, the residential developer may initiate the subdivision process. The characteristic subdivision procedure requires the submission of three sets of plats—sketch, preliminary, and final—to the planning board for review and approval. The first plat is a sketch drawn up by a consulting engineer for the project after he has conducted surveys of the property's boundaries, offsite sewer lines, and topography. It is essentially a rough design map of the proposed subdivision accompanied by supporting information concerning the location of drainage, surrounding owners, streets, cultural features, public easements, utility lines, and so forth. This stage provides the consulting engineer, residential developer, and planning board with an opportunity to discuss the design and concept of the subdivision informally and allows modification of the subdivision design before excessive costs have been incurred by the developer.

The time interval between land acquisition and sketch plat submittal varies, but the formal processing time of the sketch plat is fairly constant. The sketch plat review procedure originates in the township clerk's office where the plat is processed and forwarded to the planning board, usually within a week to ten days of original submission. When the planning board engineer declares the application complete, usually within one week, the plans committee classifies it and forwards it to other local and county agencies. The township environmental commission, health department, and county planning board review the sketch during the next four weeks and by the sixth to seventh week recommendations are returned to the plans committee. After consideration by the plans committee, the planning board reviews the sketch plat and makes recommendations concerning its approval or disapproval; the sketch plat is then returned to the developer, usually by the beginning of the eighth week. In practice, an additional month is typically required to incorporate the recommendations of the planning board into the sketch plat and secure municipal approval. A three-month period for sketch platting, while subject to some variation due to municipal docketting, is fairly standard for this phase of the subdivision process.

At this point in the local subdivision process, plans for the development remain rather flexible and alterations in site design, density, utility arrangements, and open space may be required by the state or local governments. Changes required by the state at this juncture, however, would supercede local requirements and would thus cease to derive any benefit from local review.

Preliminary Plat

The preliminary plat, typically drawn at a scale of 1" - 100′ as required by the subdivision ordinance, shows the dimensions of roadways and recreation areas and utility line flows. All adjacent parcels and their status of ownership are indicated. It also includes preliminary street profiles, storm drainage on site, and sanitary sewers on and off site. Sectionalization and staging schedules for major subdivisions are proposed, soil borings identifying depth to water table are recorded, and topographic-grading plans are provided. In addition, all the applications and reports of review for the preceding step are included as supportive material. This agglomeration of information is essentially a refinement of the original sketch plan which was approved prior to filing for the preliminary plat application.

The second stage of the subdivision process, preliminary plat approval, is the first opportunity many regulatory and service agencies have to review plans for a proposed project. At the local level, the sewerage authority, board of fire commissioners, and environmental commission become involved at this stage of the process. The county also reviews the preliminary plans and the developer applies for state transportation access permits. Utility sources such as water, telephone, and electric companies are contacted and, although they do not have authority to review the plan, they insure that essential services will be available to future residents of the subdivision.

The application for preliminary approval to the sewerage authority must include copies of the preliminary plans and completion of a standard application form supplied by the authority. Preliminary review establishes the type of sewer system required and the terms of the installation. All major subdivisions are generally required to install sanitary sewerage systems which exclude storm water runoff. The sewerage authority either allows the developer to continue expansion or requires that the plan be modified to conform to the sewerage master plan. The sewerage authority also alerts the developer to the availability of sewerage facilities for his subdivision. The time period for preliminary sewerage approval, the first of three required sewer applications, varies between one and two months depending upon the amount of time that passes before the application is placed on the municipal docket. Most approvals seem to be automatic as long as the residential developer is willing to provide on site facilities at his own expense.[10]

Review of the plat by the board of fire commissioners is also a prerequisite to a planning board decision on the preliminary plat. The fire commissioners examine subdivision plans to make certain street designs allow efficient routing of emergency vehicles and provide for an adequate number of water mains, hydrants, and alarm systems. The board also checks street names to eliminate any confusion arising from potential duplication. The fire commission deals primarily with the developer's engineer in reviewing the plan. The fire commission interacts in the subdivision process only during refinement of the preliminary plat prior to review by the planning board. The residential developer pays only consulting engineering costs for this review; usually no governmental fees are imposed here. Review of the plan by the fire commission takes approximately one month.

The third of the preliminary local reviews is conducted by the environmental commission. This agency administers a series of four environmental permits. Wetland and floodplain permits must be applied for if developments encroach upon these critical areas. However, more often than not, the residential developer will eliminate subdivision lots that fall within critical areas rather than be subjected to their permit requirements. The two remaining permits administered by the environmental commission are the land disturbance and the tree removal permits. The land disturbance permit requires submission of a soil erosion and sediment control plan, which relies heavily upon data accumulated by the local soil conservation district. The plan includes natural and disturbed contour maps of the project site, along with installation schedules which detail the erosion control measures to be employed. The developer must demonstrate that adequate provisions for surface water retention and drainage to protect exposed soil surfaces have been made. Tree removal applications must include diagrams illustrating all trees on a site and identifying those trees slated for removal. The review process is often a series of negotiations between the local conservation officer, frequently a member of the environmental commission, and the consultant for the developer. The tree removal ordinance complements the land disturbance ordinance in imposing controls to curb soil erosion and preserve vegetational amenities. The processing time necessary for environmental commission approval is approximately eleven months.

Materials and decisions generated by the sewerage authority, fire commission, and environmental commission are assimilated into the review of the preliminary plat by the local planning board. Prior to any formal action on the preliminary plat by the local planning board, county planning board approval must be obtained.

Preliminary plat review by the county[11] requires submission of plat maps and completed application forms. The county engineer assesses the drainage system and compares it to county guidelines, which frequently require estimating the costs of future drainage facilities which will be borne by those who will require these services—initially, the developer and subsequently, the housing consumer. Further evaluation may be necessary if the subdivision abuts a county road. Permits are required for road attachment and right-of-way. The county planning board acts in an advisory capacity to the township when county facilities are not directly impacted by the proposed subdivision and has definite regulatory powers if they are. The county engineer, the county planning board, and the developer's engineer frequently participate in this initial review of preliminary plans for the proposed subdivision. One month is the usual time required for the county to process preliminary subdivision plans.

At the municipal level, the period required to assemble the initial reviews usually takes three months. The application is filed with the clerk and forwarded within a week to the planning board engineer for completion; often the developer's consultant will have to furnish additional information at this point. This review is usually completed a month after the plat is submitted to the clerk. The period required by the developer's consultants to meet the deficiencies in the original preliminary plat application is quite variable. However, assuming the developer is prompt, his engineer may often meet design deficiencies within two months. During the fourth month after submission of the preliminary plat to the township clerk, the amended plat is reviewed by the planning board. Immediately after notification from the planning board engineer that the application is on the board's agenda, the developer must file a copy of the plat for public inspection and publish notice of the public hearing. Sufficient notice for the public hearing is considered to be ten days; thus, the notification period represents a substantial segment of the fifth month following preliminary plat submission to the clerk. During the week preceding the hearing, the plans committee considers the preliminary plat and makes recommendations to the planning board. At the public hearing conducted before the planning board, public agencies and individuals comment on the proposed subdivision. The planning board usually defers its decision to the next meeting, into the sixth month, to allow time for consideration of the proposed subdivision. During the next official meeting following the public hearing, the planning board either approves, disapproves, or reserves decision on the plat pending compliance with specific conditions. The approved and signed plat is usually delivered to the developer by the end of the sixth or the beginning of the seventh month. The developments in the Dover Township sample exhibited an average preliminary plat processing time of seven months, although the state enabling legislation and the corresponding local ordinances suggest a period of three months for this process.[12] Much of the additional time may be attributed to the necessity of amending the original preliminary plat and alleviating the deficiencies of the original submission.

Tentative plat approval, the term assigned to municipal approval of the preliminary plat, guarantees the residential developer that the terms and conditions of approval will not be changed for a period of three years. The developer may submit a more detailed final plat in stages within the three-year period as long as each section in the final plat meets the standards for improvements and is in general accord with the overall design of the preliminary plat.

The granting of tentative plat approval at the termination of the preliminary plat processing is a significant step in local development processing. It is at this juncture that the two participants in the process, developer and municipality, are guaranteed by law that each will honor his obligation for a period of three years. The site as planned is frozen for mutual protection.

It is important to understand the finality of the plat at this point if the local subdivision process is to be interrupted and the various developments subjected to state review. State participation subsequent to this point is legally questionable in terms of effecting changes in proposed development. Even if some way could be found to circumvent the legal relationship which exists between developer and municipality at this juncture, changes in site design, density, utility arrangements, etc., required in order to comply with state regulation dictate an increase in the duration of the development processing period, because these site refinements which have already been processed must be reassessed by the municipality.

The cost of the preliminary platting procedure is greater and involves many more participants than any of the other steps in the subdivision process. Fees are levied against the project from a number of sources—consulting engineers, architects, and environmentalists, attorneys, and government agencies. Besides being the most expensive step in the subdivision process, the preliminary plat process is probably the most unpredictable.

Final Plat[13]

The application for final approval of the plat must be submitted to the township clerk within three years of tentative approval. The submission may occur while various approvals are being sought from higher governmental agencies. The planning board, however, will reserve action on the plat pending receipt of upper level approvals. The tentatively approved preliminary plat and supplemental materials form the basis for the final plat application. The plat plans are submitted in final form according to state specifications for each section of the subdivision. The plans usually include legends, tax map block and lots, grading plans, drainage plans, detailed utility layouts, plans and comments from all previous reviews, street designs, easements, open space, and rights-of-way names.[14]

Whereas the general terms and conditions which relate to lot layout, road patterns, and design of the preliminary plat may not be changed, requirements for improvements are negotiated during the final platting sequence.[15] The plat drawings and supporting documents constitute a complete history of the proposed subdivision and become the basis for its construction.

The participants in the third platting process are essentially the same as in prior stages; minor roles are eliminated, however, as the final plat does not require a public hearing. The local planning board reviews final plat information in a much more abbreviated form than was the case for the preliminary plat. The exclusion of the public hearing and attendant notifications eliminates approximately two months from processing time.

Final platting commences with a submission to the township clerk who usually forwards the plat to the planning board engineer within a week. By the end of the first month, the plat has been reviewed, processed, and returned to the developer's engineer pending certain technicalities and minor corrections. Using the sample from Dover Township, New Jersey, as an indication, deficiencies in the final plat are corrected within two to three months and shortly thereafter, the application is declared complete. It is then placed on the docket for the next planning board meeting. As in the preliminary plat procedure, the plans committee reviews the plat and makes a recommendation to the planning board one week prior to the board meeting. During the fourth or by the fifth month, the plat is reviewed by the planning board and a decision is rendered. According to enabling legislation and ordinances, the entire process is supposed to take forty-five days from submission to approval, but complications often arise in utility negotiations, agency approvals, or bonding arrangements. In practice, the procedure for final plat approval frequently spans five months.

The cost of final platting excluding bonding is nearly the same as that for preliminary approvals. There are, however, significant changes in the distribution of costs. For example, fees for engineers constitute a larger share of the total expenses; fees for attorneys and government agencies are less. Governmental fees levied during this phase of the subdivision process are usually based on the number of buildable lots in the project; attorneys generally charge the developer at an hourly rate; and engineers may employ either option.

Although on rare occasions improvements may be installed prior to final plat application, the municipality offers the option of posting a performance bond in lieu of immediate installation. This practice allows the developer ninety days to post the several bonds required for final subdivision approval. Bonds must be secured for the improvements dictated on the final plat and for those required by the sewerage authority and shade tree commission. Both municipal and sewer system improvement bonds are based upon constantly updated rate schedules maintained by the planning board and sewerage authority. The bond for shade tree requirements is established by the local shade tree or environmental commission and rates are based on charges for trees and planting. Performance bonding assures the local government of adequate capital to construct improvements required by the final plat, should the developer fail to provide the facilities. The bonding technique keeps the developer's investment at a minimum, prior to obtaining final plat approval. Ninety days after final plat approval, bonds must be posted and accepted by the township committee. In extenuating circumstances, the township may extend the bonding period for an additional three months. Bonding is usually the last regulation to be met prior to filing the plat and commencing land conversion. When the bonds are posted with the township and all approvals are packaged, the developer files the final plat with the county recording office within ninety days of final planning board approval.

The Multifamily Case

The procedure for single-family subdivision is very similar to the procedure for multifamily development. The regulatory process for residential developments proposed as site plans, shown in Figure 15, basically combines the preliminary and final platting procedures into a single step. The process of acquiring supplemental local approvals, a portion of the single-family subdivision preliminary plat review, proceeds concurrently with site plan review. The site plan regulations require compliance with, essentially, the same set of criteria applied to single-family plat applications. The format and procedures are simplified, however, because in multifamily developments the tract of land is not subdivided into lots.

Site plan review involves the residential developer, the planning board, the engineers for both, and private citizens who participate through public hearings. In cases in which the land had been originally zoned for single-family development, application for rezoning is made to the zoning board of adjustment and that body automatically refers the site plan to the planning board at a regularly scheduled meeting. Approximately one month after the referral, the planning board engineer completes a technical review and sends notice of deficiencies to the developer's engineer. Deficiencies are corrected, usually within a period of three months, reviewed by the planning board engineer, and placed on the board's agenda. The week before the board's meeting, the plans committee meets and makes a recommendation to the full board. By the fifth month, the planning board meeting is held and, within another month, the board forwards a recommendation to the zoning board of adjustment. Following notice, a public hearing is held concerning the reasons for which a variance is being granted. This occurs during the seventh month following original submission. The attorney for the board of adjustment prepares a resolution for the next meeting, whereupon the decision of the board is made public. The site plan procedure is usually completed in eight months.

While the plan review and variance procedures are taking place, final approvals are secured for the various county, environmental, and local sewerage authority permits. These approvals are prerequisites for final approval of the site plan by the township committee or governing body. Bonding and filing procedures, regulations, and deadlines with the exception of shade tree bonding, make no distinction between the single-family and multifamily residential development.

Whereas the subdivision process is somewhat more simple for multifamily developments, the practice of proposing multifamily uses in single-family zones necessitates variance procedures, thus complicating the site plan review process and making it almost as time-consuming as that for single-family developments.

SUMMARY AND APPLICABILITY OF PREVIOUS ANALYSIS

The descriptive analysis presented in the preceding section illustrates the diffused nature of the residential subdivision process, and the difficult coordinating task faced by the local planning board. As new regulations are devised and superimposed on the existing process, legislated time periods for development reviews are extended. Less obvious variables such as staff vacations and docket scheduling also affect processing time.

The diagrams illustrating the standard subdivision process (Figures 13 and 14) are refined in this section by the introduction of a time factor which assumes the most efficient method of complying with the local land-use regulatory system. (See Figures 16 and 17.) The gaps between permit filings provide an indication of the time required to prepare subsequent applications and assemble supporting documents. Figures 16 and 17 may be considered a reasonable illustration of the subdivision process as it might appear in the coastal zones of most states. It should be emphasized, however, that individual projects can and definitely do deviate from this norm.

FIGURE 16

STANDARD SUBDIVISION PROCESS
VIEWED OVER TIME

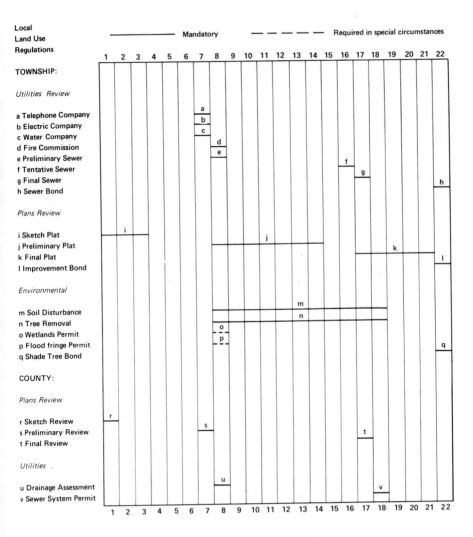

Project Duration (months)

FIGURE 17

STANDARD SITE PLAN PROCESS
VIEWED OVER TIME

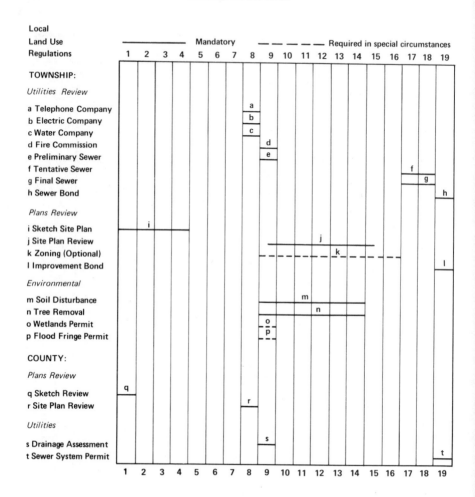

Project Duration (months)

The sample developments examined indicate that processing time for single-family development applications is twenty-two months and for multifamily developments, nineteen months.

The subdivision and site plan review process examined in this chapter represent the context in which state coastal zone management programs must operate. The costs of such intervention will be examined in a subsequent chapter.

NOTES

1. Blumenfeld, 1975, p. 7.
2. Office of Environmental Analysis, 1974, p. 6.
3. Environmental Quality Committee, 1972.
4. Burgweger, Jr., 1975, pp. 4-6.
5. Burgweger, Jr., 1975, p. 7.
6. Reilly, 1973, p. 181.
7. Office of Environmental Analysis, 1974, p. 4.
8. Bernstein and Bernstein, 1971, p. 94.
9. Goodman and Freund, 1968, pp. 442-484; Yearwood, 1971, pp. 82-87; Bernstein and Bernstein, 1971, pp. 78-88.
10. Dover Sewerage Authority, 1971, pp. 4-8; Broome, 1975, personal communication.
11. State transportation permitting authority is analogous to county responsibilities. The state authority becomes operative only when a proposed subdivision abuts a state highway. The review essentially mirrors that done by the county since it examines primarily access and drainage aspects of the preliminary plans. Minor permits are also required for road attachment, use of right-of-way, and utility opening. These regulations are designed to protect state highways from poorly planned development of adjacent land. The permits are administered by the State Department of Transportation through a series of district offices. Plans are submitted by the developer's engineer and are processed in about six months. The permits are required before construction can begin but are not a prerequisite to preliminary plat approval.

State water supply and sewerage system permitting is required in particular circumstances. A series of water supply permits regulate well drilling, water systems constructed for individual sub-

divisions of at least fifty units and surface/ground water
diversions. Sewerage system permitting commonly applies to septic systems servicing subdivisions with fifty units or more. Individual septic systems are regulated in areas at or below ten feet
in elevation. The state's coastal zone is divided up into a group of
drainage basins and each has its own set of criteria utilized for
permit reviews. Since the coastal municipalities are becoming increasingly supplied with sewers as a result of federal regional
sewerage treatment programs, the Jersey shore will eventually entertain only sewered developments, which already predominate in
Dover Township. These policies will minimize the number of developments falling under state sewerage system regulations
(Marine Sciences Center, 1975).

12. Division of State and Regional Planning, 1969.

13. The county planning board conducts a third and final review of the
proposed subdivision during the final stages of preliminary plat approval for the same purpose and in the same manner as the preliminary review. Drainage assessments, levied during the preliminary review and platting, are due prior to final county approval. These assessments, originally requiring financial
considerations from the residential developer, are often waived by
arrangements whereby the county supplies materials and the developer supplies labor for the installation of drainage pipe. Sewer
permits are also issued by the county automatically when final
local sewerage authority approval is obtained. The final county
plan review process involves the same personnel as those engaged
in the original review and, since the county was represented at the
local public hearing, no unforeseen modifications are likely to in-
terfere with the processing of the final plat. However, if the preliminary plat originally approved by the county has been substantially revised, a new preliminary submittal may be required prior
to action on the final submission. The processing times for county
plat reviews are always one month except in unusual
circumstances (Ocean County Board of Chosen Freeholders,
1970, pp. 15-17). The cost of this review includes engineering fees,
assessments for drainage, and charges for final sewer permits.

There are two stages in the sewerage authority permitting procedure during this step in the subdivision process. The first stage,

or tentative permitting, may be accomplished after the consulting engineer has drawn up the layout and profiles for the sewers allowing him to estimate the cost of improvements. The estimates for subdividing sewerage facilities follow the size, locational, and discharge guidelines in the sanitary sewer master plan and the authority regulations. The tentative platting process allows negotiation between the developer and the sewerage authority regarding the guidelines and obligations of the two parties. This interaction occurs during the month needed for tentative approval of the sewer plan and frequently is concurrent with the issuance of a final sewer permit. Permit fees typically are based on 1 percent of the proposed sewer project costs and the consulting engineering charges are limited to the charges for estimates derived from the sewer facilities plan.

The final sewer permit application requires revised negotiated plans for the subdivision's sewerage facilities and a schedule for their installation. This permit authorizes construction of the sewer lines and requires payment of a connection fee for each buildable lot in the subdivision that is to be tied in with an existing treatment plant of adequate capacity. The participants and processing time are the same for all the sewer permits. The residential developer pays a final permit fee of 1.5 percent of the sewer project costs and the consulting engineer bills him for plan revision and scheduling of construction. Nearly all residential developments also pay a $250/unit connection fee.

The State Department of Environmental Protection administers two standard environmental permits controlling subdivision of floodplains and wetlands. Both these permits reinforce and supercede the township wetlands and floodplains permits, if the municipal regulations are less restrictive. Responsibilities for regulation of residential development in the floodplain are equally delegated between local and state government. Local environmental commissions, which have the authority, restrict subdivision of the floodfringe area of the floodplain. Where the locality fails to enact an ordinance regulating floodfringe land use, the Division of Water Resources will assume the task of floodfringe regulation in addition to its control of floodway development. A permit application requires extensive information including subdivision plans, a

myriad of hydrologic calculations, findings concerning suscep-
tability of proposed activity to flood, and impact of development
on the floodplain. The reviewing agencies include all governmental bodies involved in the platting process plus the soil conservation district and county park commission. The procedure frequently requires a three-month processing period.

The approval packages from the county, local sewerage authority,
and state when processed simultaneously normally require about
three months unless the subdivider attempts to obtain a state environmental permit, in which case the time required is doubled. In
order to proceed to the final platting procedure, the permits which
were requested by the developer during the second phase of the
process must be issued. As a result, the developer's engineer must
also contact the local environmental commission and state
transportation department to obtain the wetlands, soil disturbance, tree removal, floodplain, road access, and road drainage
permits reviewed prior to preliminary platting. This assemblage of
prerequisite approvals allows the developer to apply for the third
and final plat.

14. Division of State and Regional Planning, 1969, p. 16.
15. Bernstein and Bernstein, 1971, p. 87.

Chapter 6
Coastal Zone Management Implementation: Impact on Local Land Conversion Procedures

NEW JERSEY'S COASTAL ZONE
MANAGEMENT PROGRAM ORGANIZATION

The Department of Environmental Protection (DEP) has primary responsibility for coastal zone management in New Jersey. The same department has regulatory responsibility for air and water pollution, solid waste, water supply, and radiation, and has the traditional conservation responsibility for parks, forests, fish, game, shellfisheries, open space, recreation, navigation, and marine services. Since its formation in 1970, this environmental agency has been given additional regulatory authority in the areas of noise abatement, floodplain management, pesticide control, and regulation of development in coastal wetlands. The department is also involved in the administration of state-owned riparian lands which are or fomerly were, flowed by tidal waters.

The organization of the department (Figure 18) reflects its broad charge to protect and conserve valuable natural resources. New Jersey's DEP can be designated a "superagency" as discussed in Chapter II. Superagencies not only incorporate the planning function authorized by the federal coastal zone legislation but also exercise regulatory powers authorized by state legislation. In New Jersey's superagency, an Office of Coastal Zone Management within the Division of Marine Services is responsible for both the planning and regulatory aspects of coastal zone management. While the authority to review and decide on permit applications has been delegated to the director of the Division of Marine Services, the environmental commissioner retains responsibility for long-range planning.[1]

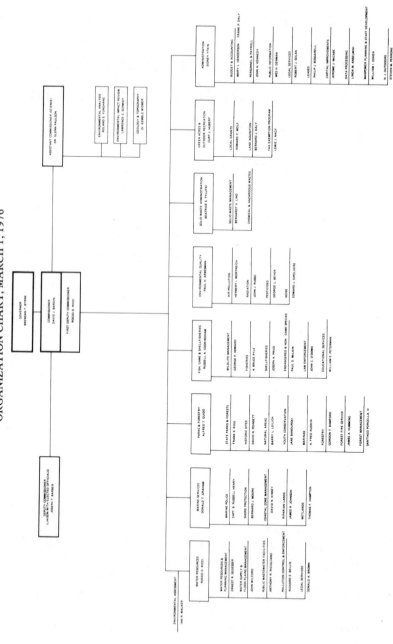

FIGURE 18
STATE OF NEW JERSEY
DEPARTMENT OF ENVIRONMENTAL PROTECTION
ORGANIZATION CHART, MARCH 1, 1976

HISTORY

New Jersey's concern for its coastal zone resources was apparent prior to creation of the DEP. A commission was organized in the late 1960s during the term of Governor Hughes with specific intent to develop a master plan for the state's coastal zone. This initial effort fell short in its attempts to come to grips with coastal problems, but subsequent actions proved more fruitful. During 1970, the state's administration of riparian rights permits underwent a transformation—from a policy of liberal conveyances to what currently amounts to a moriatorium on private acquisition of riparian land rights. Passage of the Wetlands Act (N.J.S.A. 13:9A-1) during the same year set the stage for regulation of development activities affecting coastal marshlands. At the national level, disparate federal concerns were synthesized in the Coastal Zone Management Act of 1972 (P.L. 92-583). Soon after, the New Jersey legislature, stimulated by Delaware's ban on industrial development from its coastal zone[2] enacted the Coastal Area Facility Review Act (CAFRA) of 1973 (N.J.S.A. 13:19-1). The CAFRA legislation, a derivative of federal antecedents, mandated an environmental inventory of the state's coastal zone and development of a strategy to manage coastal activities. It also went a step further by providing an interim, yet potentially permanent, implementation instrument with which DEP could regulate major commitment of scarce coastal resources.

With the grant provision of Section 305 of the Coastal Zone Management Act, New Jersey's coastal zone planning program, so essential to the administration of DEP's regulatory function in coastal areas, became operational. The first-year federal program development grant allowed DEP to increase its planning staff and organize a federally funded coastal zone management project. The DEP staff has concentrated on formulating an environmental inventory to meet the state statutory requirements and assembling an extensive data base for the preparation of guidelines to direct the state's evolving coastal zone management system.[3] The state legislature itself performed the first coastal planning task by defining a boundary for the coastal zone. Many of the other substantive elements of program formulation discussed in Chapter II, such as delineation of critical areas and definition of permissible uses and their priority, were originally deferred pending completion of the inventory. The urgency of the need to regulate

coastal development activities, however, has compelled an accelera-
tion of the planning process, and the staff has turned its attention to developing additional substantive program elements immediately upon
completion of the inventory. Furthermore, the regulatory agency's
need for some type of management scheme upon which to base interim
land-use decisions has led to the development of temporary guidelines
for coastal development activities.

The interagency coordination, information dissemination, and
public participation elements mandated by the Coastal Zone Management Act are also underway within New Jersey's coastal zone program. To assist the DEP, a CAFRA Task Force, consisting of
representatives of all the relevant agencies of state government, has
been organized. Intergency coordination is also incorporated into the
administration of the regulatory function in the form of statutory membership of the Department of Community Affairs and the Department
of Labor and Industry in the appellate Coastal Area Review Board. Information concerning coastal zone management is disseminated
through the Office of the Commissioner. Public participation has been
encouraged through a series of workshops and public advisory coun-
cils, methods utilized by many coastal states.

The state's authority and ability to implement its coastal zone
management program has proven to be a most sensitive problem for
New Jersey, as in other states seeking Section 306 administrative
grants.[4]

NEW JERSEY'S COASTAL LAND-USE REGULATIONS

The New Jersey Department of Environment Protection employs
three basic regulations to carry out its objectives in the coastal area.
The implementation of coastal zone management in New Jersey emphasizes CAFRA (Appendix D), Wetlands, and Riparian Rights
permitting procedures (Figure 19).[5] The most encompassing of the
coastal regulatory measures is the Coastal Area Facility Review Act
(CAFRA), which requires exhaustive socioeconomic and environmental review of large-scale development proposals within critical as well
as noncritical areas of the coastal zone. It formally directs the Department of Environmental Protection to regulate industrial land uses and
residential developments of twenty-five units or more between the
shoreline and specified inland roads and railroads. CAFRA further

FIGURE 19

NEW JERSEY'S REGULATED COASTAL AREA

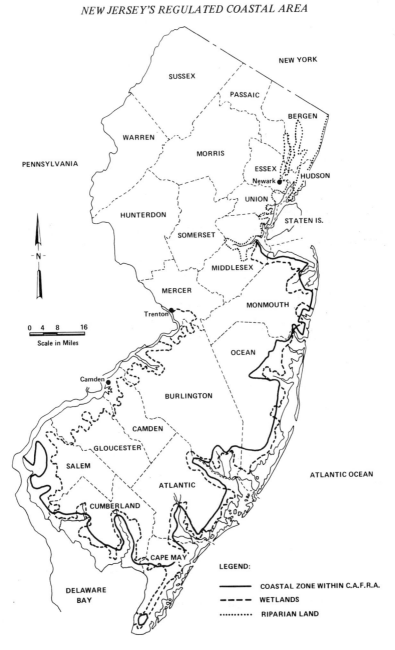

authorized DEP to review and regulate marine terminals and cargo facilities, installation of above and underground pipelines designed to transport petroleum, natural gas, and sanitary sewage, electric power generating, food processing, waste incineration, paper production, agrichemical production, chemical processing, storage, metallurgical processing, sanitary landfills, waste treatment plants, and highway construction.[6]

The CAFRA legislation requires the DEP to review projects proposing any of the above uses on an *ad hoc* basis during a minimum three-year period, pending completion of a management plan. The state law, paralleling national coastal zone management guidelines, further establishes three requisites for the new program. Within one year subsequent to a two-year environmental inventory of coastal resources, the DEP planning staff is to prepare a series of alternative long-range coastal zone management strategies. During the fourth year, a development plan, balancing the need to preserve environmental objectives against economic and social pressures, is to be formulated from one, or a synthesis of the several, alternative management strategies. The plan, to be submitted to the governor and the legislature, is scheduled for completion in September 1977.

Regulatory authority drawn from the coastal zone legislation is embodied in a permit procedure which requires developers of major facilities to submit an application form, an environmental impact statement, and such additional information as the environmental commissioner may require, prior to the initiation of site preparation (P.L. 1973, Chapter 185-N.J.S.A. 13:19-1). All of these elements constitute various parts of the CAFRA application. In addition the CAFRA application must include: the name and address of the applicant, a written explanation of the proposed facility including a future activities plan, a list of adjacent land owners, a map locating the proposed project within its locale, the preliminary plat map with all supplementary data, certification of ownership of interest in the property, and an environmental impact statement.

Purpose

The purpose of CAFRA is identical to that of the federal Coastal Zone Management Act of 1972; namely, to balance competing activities, to protect against additional adverse effects, to prevent resource exhaustion, to regulate further construction, to protect the fragile and sensitive areas of the coast, to preserve the capacity of the zone, to respond to multiple and diverse uses, and to address these goals from local, regional, and statewide perspectives. In addition, the CAFRA legislation is intended to encourage alternative development options in the coastal zone by limiting the scope of development prior to the establishment of standards by the state's coastal zone management program. The dilemma has always been discouraging resource-degrading developments while providing for economically necessary, nondetrimental ones.

The Review Process

The CAFRA review process, which is not yet formalized, now involves most divisions of the Department of Environmental Protection (Figure 18) as well as elements of the Departments of Community Affairs and Labor and Industry. Requiring submission of the permit application allows the DEP to distribute complete sets of the document to all interested agencies so that reviews may proceed simultaneously. By statute, the DEP commissioner is responsible for the evaluation and issuance of CAFRA permits, but actual project review and permit authority has been delegated to the director of the Division of Marine Services. This division is responsible for coordination of all agency reviews, public hearings, and evaluations of applications. Results of these activities in the form of draft reports with attendant recommendations filter from the section supervisor through the planning coordinator to the division director, who decides whether to approve, conditionally approve, or deny an application. As a matter of policy, the environmental staff solicits a maximum of critical comment prior to making a decision on the CAFRA application.

The CAFRA process consists of five stages, beginning with a residential developer's request for a preapplication conference. This request may be made at the same time that the sketch plat is submitted to local authorities or any time thereafter. A preapplication conference furnishes the developer with a docket number, review process timetable, and checklist of regulations potentially applicable to the proposed project. The applicant may furnish the department with a general plan of his project analogous to the sketch plat. Following the preapplication conference, the developer may also be required to publish notice of intent to file for a coastal zone permit, whereupon he must provide information to the public concerning his organization, the proposed project, the specific local government agency wherein the application may be found and reviewed, the permit docket number, and the state regulatory agency to which the public may submit written comments regarding their view of the application. An affidavit of distribution and certification of notice of publication then becomes a prerequisite addendum to the formal application.

The actual review process commences with the receipt of the formal application by the CAFRA section of the Office of Coastal Zone Management. Copies of the application are immediately distributed to the Department of Labor and Industry, the Department of Community Affairs, and the Divisions of Environmental Quality, Water Resources, Parks and Forestry, and Fish, Game, and Shellfisheries. In reviewing the permit application, written comments from the public and governmental agencies are taken into consideration if received within the first three weeks subsequent to submission. By the fourth week, the applicant is notified about the completeness of his application;[7] nearly all applications require additional information. The time usually necessary to amend an application is approximately two months. After an additional two weeks—or by the midpoint of the fourth month of the permit-process—the amended application is filed and a public hearing is scheduled. Various state agencies are required to prepare analyses of the application and the Division of Marine Services drafts a preliminary decision on the application in the one- to two-month interim preceding the public hearing.

Responsibilities for notification of the public hearing are split between the developer and the DEP. Both give public notice fifteen days prior to the hearing, DEP publishes particulars of the public hearings, whereas the applicant alerts adjoining landowners and local regulatory agencies. Usually during the sixth month of the process, the commissioner's designee holds a quasilegislative or nonadversary public hearing to afford interested parties, including the applicant, an opportunity to comment on the proposed project and the environmental commissioner's preliminary analysis. The hearing record remains open for the succeeding fifteen days to entertain additional written comments, and after this period the department frequently requires the developer to submit final supplementary information. During the seventh month the applicants submit additional requested data; all information is then scrutinized during the final three month review.

The next stage of review spans a period of two to five months and culminates in issuance or denial of a permit. When additional information is requested from the developer subsequent to the public hearing, the state regulatory agency may take three instead of two months to arrive at a decision. Based on the experience of the first year and a half of the law's operation, the commissioner's decision is normally released by the tenth month. The permit, however, is not issued until a three-week intervenor period has elapsed; the purpose of this period is to provide interested parties with an opportunity to comment or contest the decision. In practice, this period may add an eleventh and even a twelfth month to the permitting process.

ALTERATION OF THE LOCAL SUBDIVISION PROCESS AS A RESULT OF CAFRA

State coastal zone management controls must obviously interact with the standard subdivision review process. As such they permanently superimpose an additional level of government regulations onto an already complex and time-consuming process. New Jersey's implementation of the Coastal Area Facility Review Act provides one of the few opportunities to monitor the impact of interim state coastal zone regulation on the local subdivision process prior to the formulation of a permanent regulatory policy.

State review of development permits in the coastal zone was originally to take place after the development application had been processed at the local level. Thus, the time for state review, ten to twelve months, was added directly to the existing two-year local development review period. However, this administrative policy was found to be inappropriate soon after the coastal zone program was underway. Instead, state entrance in the process has now been occurring at the point at which information is being gathered for preliminary plat submission. As a result, concurrent, state and local reviews now span a period of two years and terminate with final plat approval at the local level. Figure 20 depicts the current subdivision process as it has been altered by state intervention. The process still includes the standard sequence of local submissions but the initiation of final plat application occurs two months further along in the process. Thus, two years are required for what was, previously, a twenty-two month local platting se-

FIGURE 20

THE SUBDIVISION PROCESS VIEWED OVER TIME,
AS ALTERED BY STATE INTERVENTION

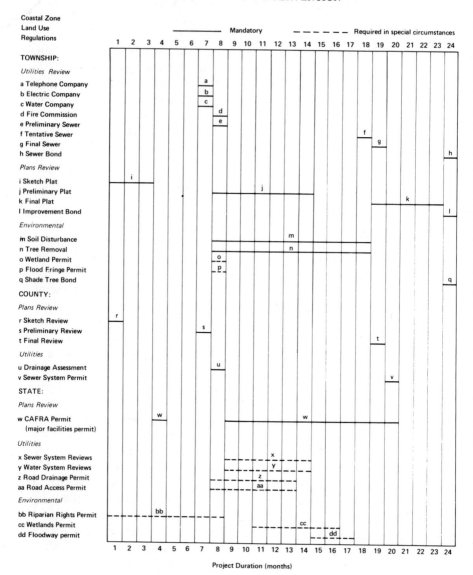

Project Duration (months)

FIGURE 21

THE SITE PLAN PROCESS VIEWED OVER TIME, AS ALTERED BY STATE INTERVENTION

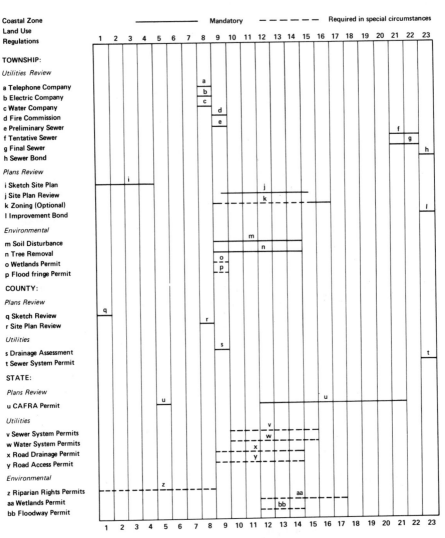

Project duration (months)

quence. Notwithstanding the two-month delay as a result of the CAFRA requirement, local reviews have retained both their administrative and procedural integrity.

The current process for regulating multifamily developments (Figure 21) is a refinement of the local site plan review process. The diagram for site plan review includes allocations of time for obtaining a use variance; however, this review requires a minimum of six months regardless of the project's initial zoning status.

CAFRA's impact on the multifamily site plan review process becomes apparent by comparing the CAFRA-altered sequence, as illustrated in Figure 21, with the standard multifamily process illustrated in Figure 17. Application for a CAFRA permit may be made concurrently with submission of plans for local site plan review—the stage immediately following sketch plat approval in the multifamily process. With the CAFRA regulations in effect, the traditional nineteen-month site plan review period is extended to twenty-three months. As in the case of single-family subdivisions, the internal structure of the local sequence remains intact.

Up to this point, only the increases in processing time resulting from the CAFRA legislation have been considered. However, other factors have also been affected. For example, a subtle modification has occurred as a result of increased sensitivity on the part of both the state and local governments for the integrity of each other's roles. Local governments have grown to depend almost exclusively on the state for environmental impact guidelines; at the same time, the previous tendency on the part of the state to put too much emphasis on controlling site design has been mitigated.

NOTES

1.   Kinsey, 1975, personal communication.
2.   Governor's Task Force on Marine and Coastal Affairs, 1972.
3.   Bardin, 1975, p. 4.
4.   Schwaderes, May 21, 1975, p. 2.
5.   See the appendix which follows this chapter.
6.   Commercial development is not specifically addressed in the act, however, DEP maintains it has authority to review such facilities in a fashion similar to its regulation of residential and industrial de-

velopment. Considerable controversy rages over this interpretation and court challenge may be imminent due to ambiguities in the drafted legislation.

7.   Dryla, 1975, personal communication.

APPENDIX TO CHAPTER 6
THE INTERACTION OF
WETLANDS AND RIPARIAN RIGHTS
WITH CAFRA
IN THE COASTAL ZONE

Wetlands

The Wetlands Act of 1970 (P.L. 1970, Chap. 272-N.J.S.A. 13:9A-1) authorizes the Department of Environmental Protection, over a two year period, to delineate all coastal wetlands within the state and set up a permit system for regulating activities in an effort to prevent their further deterioration. Pursuant to this Act, wetlands maps were developed based on twenty-six species of plants considered characteristic of marsh vegetation communities. Activities in the wetlands, as defined by the species inventory, are restricted by a two-tiered permitting system. An abbreviated review process for Type-A permits covers projects which are considered to have a rather insignificant impact on coastal wetlands. Type-B permits for projects necessitating construction, excavation, or dredge and fill require a public hearing and submission of a detailed application and/or environmental impact statement.

Recognition of the public worth of estuarine marshlands fostered regulation of its dredging, filling, and alteration. As such, the development rights to these wetlands have been essentially confiscated by the state for the benefit of the citizenry. For residential lagoon housing development, this legislation is more of a moratorium than a regulatory device. A section within the Division of Marine Services administers the state's wetland reviews in much the same manner as the CAFRA Section in the Office of Coastal Zone Management evaluates CAFRA applications. Within one month of a submission for wetlands permit the regulatory agency is required to review an application for deficiencies. When these deficiences are met, the section has fifteen days to review the amended application for completeness. When the submission is complete and filed, a public hearing is scheduled within one to two months of that date. The Department may request a final submission of additional information during the fifteen days subsequent to the hearing and is allowed three months to render a decision on the project. The whole procedure from submission to issuance of a permit requires at least three and possibly up to ten months. Costs are not limited to the developer's legal agent and consulting engineer. A government fee of one half of 1 percent of construction costs is levied for both Type-A and Type-B permit applications (Hampton, 1975, personal communication).

Riparian Rights

New Jersey is one of thirty-one Eastern riparian states which base private rights to the use of water flowing in water courses and coastal areas on ownership of riparian land contiguous to that water. Riparian law covers water as well as land (R.S.12:3-1 et. seg.). Jurisdiction applies to those lands along natural waterways, which are or were formerly inundated permanently or periodically by tidal waters at and below the line of mean high tide. The state owns, unless it has previously conveyed its interests, all riparian lands including those filled or reclaimed without a grant, lease, license, or permit. Even after such lands have been conveyed to private interests, the state retains regulatory control over their use in the form of waterfront development permitting. For the northeast region of the state, riparian law is presently the sole implementation instrument of coastal zone management (Marine Sciences Center, 1975).

A residential developer must purchase by grant or rent by lease, license, or easement riparian rights from the state if an improvement is anticipated. For residential housing, a grant and construction permit (R.S. 12:5-3, 12:5-6) are required. An application for these instruments consists of eight elements: 1) a metes and bounds description of the adjacent upland including multiple copies of a land survey indicating adjoining landowners, water width and depth at low and high tide respectively, the mean high water line, and federal pierhead or bulkhead lines; 2) a description of the proposed improvement and any previous privileges conveyed by the state; 3) definition of the type of conveyance sought; 4) copies of deed and certificate of title to the upland; 5) statement concerning the type of firm making application; 6) a designation of any signee of the application other than the riparian landowner; 7) a filing fee; and 8) an abbreviated environmental impact statement demonstrating how the project will serve the public interest and affect the submerged land's environment. Such an application places the state under no obligation to convey its riparian rights to the applicant nor must a construction permit be issued to a previous grantee.

Prior to the advent of the Coastal Zone Management Act, the coastal states acted as trustees of riparian lands, frequently raising revenue through their disposition. With the dawn of concern for the coastal area, ownership of land, including the riparian portion, has been retained by the state to assist in program implementation. In New Jersey, though previously dispersed among many agencies, riparian land management has been vested in the Bureau of Navigation and recently incorporated into the Division of Marine Services as the Riparian Section. A decision-making body, the Natural Resource Council, established the administrative policy followed by the Riparian Section. Reviews coordinated by this section include input from the Secretary of State, Secretary of Transportation, Corporate Tax Bureau in the Department of Treasury, Bureau of Land Acquisitions, and all Divisions and Commissions of the Department of Environmental Protection. Grants and leases must be signed by at least seven members of the twelve member council and then approved by the DEP commissioner, attorney general, and the governor.

Applications for grants and leases are often processed concurrently with requests for construction permits. However, these combined applications encounter different administrative policies than those in which the rights have been previously conveyed by the state and the request is limited to a development permit. The conveyance of riparian rights requires an elaborate review of titles, clearances, and vouchers and often lasts up to five months. When all documentation has been assembled, the application is placed on the docket of the Natural Resource Council where, in approximately one month's time, it is heard in an open meeting. The state's current policy has been to refuse sale of riparian rights. However, should the council pass the motion, three state officials are allowed review and may veto the council's action. Grants favorably recommended by the council require an additional 30-60 days to pass through the offices of the commissioner of DEP, the attorney general, and the governor.

In cases where only a development permit is sought (rights have already been transferred), the Riparian Section review, with referrals to other agencies, consumes about three months. A fourth month is required for council hearing and decision; a final thirty days is required to clear the DEP commissioner's review process. In contrast to an outright moratorium on rights' grants, development permits are judged on the merits of a particular project.

The riparian rights procedure is commonly part of the early stages of the subdivision process, quite possibly a component of initial land acquisition. With the moratorium on lagoon housing developments, riparian applications for residential uses have been severely curtailed. However, the development pressures for recreational and other types of facilities associated with upland activities continue to stimulate riparian applications; almost 700 applications of all classes were processed in 1975 alone. Despite this pressure from the private sector, state policy has not changed and almost no conveyances and only a limited number of construction permits are being authorized.

Governmental fees for riparian rights depend upon the type of conveyance instrument sought by the developer. Grants and leases require a $25 filing and a $100-$550 preparation fee plus payment of the land's market value based on area or frontage. A waterfront construction permit bears the same filing fee plus a minimum $100 or a 5 percent of construction costs assessment. Revenues raised through the conveyance of riparian rights must be deposited in the state school fund according to the New Jersey State Constitution, Article VIII, Section IV.

Chapter 7

The Cost of Local and State Regulation

All the figures in the following discussion will represent unadjusted costs[1] incurred by development proposals in the Dover Township, New Jersey, sample during the 1972-1975 period (Appendix B). Data for various regulations represent the means as calculated for the eleven single-family and nine multifamily cases.

DEVELOPMENT CHARACTERISTICS

Developments in the single-family sample (Table 12) represent an aggregate of 982 dwelling units on 719.7 acres, with lot sizes ranging from 7,500 to 45,000 square feet and an average density of 1.3 units per acre. The average project contains ninety units, each unit situated on a 17,000 square-foot lot, with a total site area of approximately sixty-five acres. The nine sample multifamily residential developments (Table 13) constitute an aggregate of 1,810 dwelling units on 274.2 acres; densities range from four to nine units per acre with a mean of approximately seven units per acre. The average multifamily project contains 200 units at seven units per acre on a thirty acre tract.

Both the single and multifamily samples exhibit similar size ranges, with the two largest projects in each accounting for nearly one-half the proposed dwelling units. Cost data presented here are most exemplary of single-family developments of 50-100 units and multifamily projects of the 100-200 unit variety. Although total project costs vary according to the scale of the operation, regulatory costs per unit remain fairly constant across the range of development sizes within a given housing type. Basically, this conclusion parallels the observations of Muller and James in their investigation of per unit costs related to environmental impact statements.[2]

TABLE 12

UNITS, ACREAGE AND LOT SIZE CHARACTERISTICS OF
THE SINGLE-FAMILY DEVELOPMENT SAMPLE
(Dover Township, N.J. — 1975)

Project Number	Number of Units	Number of Acres	Lot Size (sq. ft.)
1	63	32.7	17,400
2	47	34.2	18,000
3	144	78.1	18,000
4	28	7.9	7,500
5	35	11.3	12,000
6	96	43.5	15,000
7	36	18.0	14,000
8	109	39.0	9,000
9	313	400.0	45,000
10	72	44.5	20,000
11	39	10.5	11,000
Total	982	719.7	
Average	89	65.4	17,000
Range	28-313	7.9–400	7,500–45,000

TABLE 13

UNITS, ACREAGE AND LOT SIZE CHARACTERISTICS OF THE MULTIFAMILY DEVELOPMENT SAMPLE
(Dover Township, N.J. — 1975)

Project Number	Number of Units	Number of Acres	Density Per Acre
13	348	43.8	7.9
14	38	4.1	9.3
15	110	27.0	4.1
16	72	9.0	8.0
17	276	46.3	6.0
18	160	25.7	6.2
19	184	23.0	8.0
20	62	10.4	6.0
21	560	84.9	6.6
Total	1810	274.2	62.1
Average	201	30.5	6.9
Range	38-560	4.1—84.9	4.1—9.3

REGULATORY COSTS OF THE
LAND CONVERSION PROCESS

Primary contributors to regulatory costs will be indicated by the use of the designations: "E" for engineering consultants; "L" for legal counsel; and "G" for governmental regulatory fees. Capital letters indicate that a major share of the cost is attributable to this category; lower case letters represent a minor share. Tables 14 through 16 summarize the costs of governmental regulations and will be the primary references for the analysis which follows.

One basic point requires mentioning here. As one examines the number of costs associated with development processing, it must be remembered that these costs are imposed to guarantee *only* the bare essentials of public health, safety, and welfare. The public is not guaranteed creative physical design or even the most basic aspects of social and economic equity. The costs detailed here insure only that roads meet, fire equipment can maneuver, storm water does not pollute water resources, and traffic is not snarled by individual property access to a major thoroughfare. The price for even these limited achievements is considerable.

Sketch Platting

The costs of coastal zone regulations (Table 14) have been traced through the subdivision process beginning with the first of the required local processing stages, the sketch plat. Services charged to the developer for a sketch are almost exclusively rendered by a consulting engineer. Single-family developments incur fees of $58.00 and multifamily developments incur fees of $25.00 per unit for sketch plat preparation; no municipal filing fee is levied.

Preliminary Platting

The gathering of approvals as a prelude to preliminary plat approval involves the actions and resultant costs mandated by a number of regulations. Preliminary sewer plan approval, which usually costs $9.00 per unit for single-family projects and $7.00 per unit for multifamily projects, requires a basic outlay of $5.00 per unit for a municipal review fee, to which the developer's engineer adds an additional service fee. Review by the board of fire commissioners costs

TABLE 14

SUBDIVISION REGULATION COSTS IN THE COASTAL ZONE
(Dover Township, N.J. — 1975)

Regulation	Single Family		Multi-Family		Cost Sources
	Per Unit	Typical Project (100 d.u.)	Per Unit	Typical Project (100 d.u.)	
		Township:			
Sketch Plat	58.00	5,800.00			E
Preliminary Plat	127.00	12,700.00			ELg
Final Plat	127.00	12,700.00			Elg
Inspection Fees	188.00	18,800.00			G
Cash Improvement Bond	515.00	51,500.00			G
Performance Improvement Bond	54.00	5,400.00			G
Site Plan Review			25.00	2,500.00	E
Site Plan Approval			107.00	10,700.00	ELg
Zoning Variances			30.00	3,000,000	eLg
Performance Improvement Bond			28.00	2,800.00	G
Preliminary Sewer Plan	9.00	900.00	7.00	700.00	eG
Tentative Sewer Plan	11.00	1,100.00	6.00	600.00	eG
Final Sewer Plan	20.00	2,000.00	11.00	1,100.00	eG
Sewer Connection	250.00	25,000.00	250.00	25,000.00	G
Sewer Inspection	50.00	5,000.00	30.00	3,000.00	G
Cash Sewer Bond	69.00	6,900.00	53.00	5,300.00	G
Performance Sewer Bond	11.00	1,100.00	8.00	800.00	G
Water Company					
Telephone Company					
Electric Company					
Fire Commission Review	7.00	700.00	3.00	300.00	E
Soil-land Disturbance Permit	20.00	2,000.00	8.00	800.00	EG
Tree Removal Permit	16.00	1,600.00	7.00	700.00	EG
Floodplain Permit*					
Wetlands Permit*	8.00	800.00			E
Shade Tree Bond	12.00	1,300.00			eG
		County:			
Preliminary Plans Review	2.00	200.00	1.00	100.00	E
Final Plans Review	2.00	200.00	1.00	100.00	E
Drainage Assessment*	61.00	6,100.00			G
Sewer System Permit	2.00	100.00	1.00	100.00	G
		State:			

TABLE 14 (Continued)

SUBDIVISION REGULATION COSTS IN THE COASTAL ZONE
(Dover Township, N.J. — 1975)

Agency and Cost	Single Family		Multi-Family		Cost Source
	Per Unit	*Typical Project (100 d.u.)*	*Per Unit*	*Typical Project (100 d.u.)*	
CAFRA Permit	50.00	5,000.00	33.00	3,300.00	EL
Stream Encroachment Permit					
Riparian Rights Permit*			14.00	1,400.00	EL
Wetlands Permit					
Road Access Permit*	3.00	300.00	2.00	200.00	Eg
Road Drainage Permit*	3.00	300.00	2.00	200.00	Eg
Water System Review Series					
Sewer System Review Series					
TOTAL	$1,600.00	$160,000.00	$609.00	$60,400.00	

E, e —major, minor contribution of engineer or consultants
L, l —major, minor contribution of legal counsel
G, g —major, minor contribution of government fee
* —special permits not included in total

single- and multifamily developers $7.00 and $3.00 per unit, respectively, principally in engineering fees; no specific municipal levy is incurred. The final costs[3] incurred by a single-family development prior to formal preliminary plat processing include $20.00 per unit for a municipal soil disturbance permit and $16.00 per unit for a municipal tree removal permit.

In addition, engineering consultants charge the developer $2.00 per unit to present the county with plans for single-family subdivisions and $1.00 per unit for multifamily development plans. Private utilities—telephone, electric, and water—require no fee for a commitment but do levy a fee for installation. State transportation permits, if needed for residential streets, have no review fees, but the engineer who represents the developer in presenting the plans to the state charges the developer $3.00 per single-family unit and $2.00 per multifamily unit.[4]

Of the expenses incurred by single-family developments during preliminary approval, 53 percent of the total is attributable to the project's consulting engineer and 47 percent is the result of fees levied by governmental agencies (Table 15). Multifamily developments, during the equivalent stage of preliminary site plan review, incur costs distributed about equally between consultants and governmental agencies (Table 16).

The formal preparation and review of the preliminary plat or site plan results in cash outlays of $127.00 per unit for single-family developments and $107.00 per unit for multifamily developments. Platting costs for both the single-family subdivision process and the multifamily site plan review process consist of roughly the same constituents— 70 percent for engineering, 25 percent for legal, and 5 percent for governmental fees. Since review of plans requires fewer steps for multi-family developments, the cost of the plans review for the single-family subdivision process is more than that charged for the multifamily site plan review procedure. This remains true even if the multifamily development must obtain a zoning variance. The cost of obtaining a zoning variance, two-thirds of which can be assigned to legal services, averages $30.00 per unit.

Final Platting

The final approval-gathering stage of the process adds still more

TABLE 15

SINGLE-FAMILY SUBDIVISION PROCESS:
PERCENT OF TOTAL REGULATORY COSTS ATTRIBUTED TO EACH FEE SOURCE,
Dover Township, N.J., 1975

Project Number	Sketch Plat			Preliminary Approval Gathering			Preliminary Plat			Final Approval Gathering			Final Plat			CAFRA Permit		
	E	L	G	E	L	G	E	L	G	E	L	G	E	L	G	E	L	G
1	100	0	0	69 (70)	0	31 30)a	83	13	4	12	0	88	76	4	20	73 (52	27 19	0 29)b
2	100	0	0	46 (48)	0	54 52)	63	30	7	13	0	87	47	18	25	39 (33	61 52	0 15)
3	100	0	0	53 (55)	0	47 45)	57	38	5	11	0	89	62	12	26	40 (34	60 51	0 15)
4	100	0	0	57 (60)	0	43 40)	66	27	7	7	0	93	63	9	28	25 (18	75 55	0 27)
5	100	0	0	55 (58)	0	45 42)	95	0	5	25	0	75	89	0	11	79 (52	21 14	0 34)
6	100	0	0	53 (55)	0	47 45)	83	12	5	14	0	86	81	4	15	83 (70	17 15	0 15)
7	100	0	0	66 (68)	0	34 32)	77	15	8	36	0	64	73	10	17	54 (44	46 37	0 19)
8	100	0	0	56 (58)	0	44 42)	50	48	2	18	0	82	65	21	14	38 (33	62 54	0 13)
9	100	0	0	45 (47)	0	55 53)	65	21	14	23	0	77	74	11	15	11 (10	89 82	0 7)
10	100	0	0	41 (44)	0	59 56)	46	43	11	27	0	73	57	18	25	28 (21	72 53	0 26)
11	100	0	0	47 (49)	0	53 51)	62	35	3	12	0	88	71	1	16	75 (55	25 18	0 27)
Average	100	0	0	53	0	47	68	26	6	18	0	82	70	11	19	50	50	0
Range	100	0	0	41-69	0	31-59	46-95	0-48	2-4	7-36	0	64-93	57-89	0-21	11-28	17-89	18-89	0

a) cost distribution including special permits
b) cost distribution including proposed $750.00 governmental fee
E) Engineer, traffic specialists, architect, design consultant, ecologists
L) legal agent, lawyer, attorney

fees to the costs of a residential development. The greatest source of these fees are governmental levies for various required approvals. Eighty-two percent of single-family and 90 percent of multifamily development expenses incurred during the final approval phase are related to governmental requirements. The two-tiered final sewerage review costs the single-family residential developer $11.00 per unit for tentative sewer plan approval, $20.00 for final acceptance, and $50.00 for the inspection fee. Multifamily projects are assigned unit costs of $6.00, $11.00 and $30.00, respectively, for the same services. The county also plays a role in the final approval of sewerage facilities for residential development, charging a flat fee of $100.00 per review. The average for the sample of developments amounts to $2.00 per unit for single-family developments and $1.00 per unit for multifamily developments.[5]

The cost for final review of plans at the county level amounts to the same as that for the sewer permit, $2.00 per single-family unit, $1.00 per multifamily unit; however, these fees are paid to the developer's consulting engineer rather than to the county. The gathering of approvals prior to final plat submission in coastal developments costs single-family developers a total of $85.00 per unit and multifamily developers $49.00 per unit.

The formal filing of the final plat applies only to single-family subdivisions. On the average, the developer may reasonably expect to pay a fee of $127.00 per unit to secure approval of the final plat. This is identical to that required for preliminary plat filing (Table 14). Private consultants are responsible for 70 percent of this total, local government agencies 19 percent, and attorneys 11 percent (Table 15).

Following final platting and state approval, the residential developer, before sale or site preparation, must pay for posting bonds, inspection fees, and connection fees with various agencies and utilities. Single-family developers post a shade tree bond amounting to $12.00 per unit, a cash performance bond for $515.00 per unit, a surety bond of $54.00 per unit, and pay a municipal inspection fee of $188.00 per unit. Multifamily developers with site plans post only a surety performance bond which averages $28.00 per unit. Both types of residential development are charged $250.00 per unit in sewer connection fees as a requirement for final sewer plan approval. Bonding, the last step in the coastal land conversion process, is a precondition of final

TABLE 16

MULTIFAMILY SITE PLAN REVIEW PROCESS:
PERCENT OF TOTAL REGULATORY COSTS ATTRIBUTED TO EACH FEE SOURCE,
Dover Township, N.J., 1975

Project Number	Sketch Site Plan			Preliminary Approval Gathering			Site Plan Review			Zoning Variance			Final Approval Gathering			CAFRA Permit		
	E	L	G	E	L	G	E	L	G	E	L	G	E	L	G	E	L	G
13	100	0	0	30 (39)	0	70 (61)[a]	76	14	10	7	44	49	4	0	96	78 (67)	22 (19)	0 (14)[b]
14	100	0	0	58 (61)	0	42 (39)	69	29	2	5	4	91	10	0	90	56 (46)	44 (30)	0 (18)
15	100	0	0	67 (68)	0	33 (32)	78	10	12	4	76	20	17	0	83	58 (50)	42 (36)	0 (14)
16	100	0	0	66 (68)	0	34 (32)	62	36	2	11	85	4	11	0	89	35 (26)	65 (49)	0 (25)
17	100	0	0	27 (35)	0	73 (65)	88	6	6	9	85	6	3	0	97	68 (55)	32 (26)	0 (19)
18	100	0	0	61 (65)	0	39 (35)	65	32	3	5	92	3	8	0	92	50 (43)	50 (43)	0 (14)
19	100	0	0	41 (46)	0	59 (54)	62	33	5	13	72	15	14	0	86	70 (59)	30 (26)	0 (15)
20	100	0	0	58 (61)	0	42 (39)	62	34	4	6	77	17	18	0	82	49 (39)	51 (41)	0 (20)
21	100	0	0	30 (37)	0	70 (63)	68	23	9	2	72	26	4	0	96	62 (52)	38 (32)	0 (16)
Average	100	0	0	49	0	51	70	24	6	7	67	26	10	0	90	58	42	0
Range	100	0	0	27-67	0	33-73	62-88	6-32	2-12	2-13	4-92	3-91	3-18	0	82-97	35-78	22-65	0

a. cost distribution including special permits
b. cost distribution including proposed $750.00 government fee
E) Engineer, traffic specialists, architect, design consultants, ecologists
L) legal agent, lawyer, attorney
G) fees for governmental reviews, applications, and assessments

plat filing which requires cash outlays totalling $1,019.00 per single-family unit and $278.00 per multifamily unit.

THE STATE COASTAL ZONE PERMIT AS A REGULATORY COST

Activities associated with the processing of a CAFRA permit currently occasion a cost of $50.00 and $33.00 per unit for single- and multifamily developments, respectively. These permit costs may be expected to double and a major source of fees will probably shift from legal services to engineering consultants as a result of the increasing complexity of CAFRA's environmental impact statement requirements, coupled with the increasing predictability of the permitting procedure. The direct costs of obtaining a coastal zone permit ($50.00 S.F./$33.00 M.F.) currently represent 3 percent of the total per unit single-family regulatory costs ($1,600) and 5 percent of the multifamily regulatory costs ($609). These ratios may be expected to increase with the imposition of a CAFRA governmental fee of $500.00 per project and $10.00 per unit.[6] The effect on developments in the sample indicates this fee will increase the direct cost of CAFRA permitting by $19.00 per single-family unit and $15.00 per multifamily unit. Regulatory costs are combined in the next section with land, carrying, and opportunity costs in order to determine the total land conversion costs for sample residential developments in the coastal zone.

OTHER COSTS OF LAND SUBDIVISION: CALCULATING THE COSTS INVOLVED IN LAND CONVERSION

Obviously, regulations and the costs involved with their processing are not the only costs incurred by the developer in land conversion (Table 17). The cost of the land itself is the most basic item in the total expenditures by the developer. Taxes, interest charges, and opportunity costs are also incurred during the two years of regulatory processing. The total cost of land conversion is, thus, the sum of land costs plus all expenses that accrue during the subdivision process.

Land Costs

Land in the coastal zone is acquired, assembled, and financed in a

TABLE 17

COST OF THE SUBDIVISION PROCESS
(Dover Township, N.J., 1975)

	Single-family (Per unit)		Multifamily (Per unit)	
	Average	Range	Average	Range
Regulations	$1,600.00	$1,225.00 – 2,009.00	$ 609.00	$ 454.00 – 877.00
Land	2,319.00	959.00 – 3,522.00	1,276.00	441.00 – 3,473.00
Interest	201.00	5.00 – 430.00	83.00	7.00 – 245.00
Taxes	93.00	30.00 – 167.00	52.00	14.00 – 157.00
Carrying Costs				
15 percent	684.00	361.00 – 1,137.00	288.00	100.00 – 489.00
20 percent	912.00	481.00 – 1,516.00	383.00	131.00 – 652.00
Cost of Approved Land Parcel or Unit at 15% percent carrying costs	$4,897.00	$3,632.00 – 6,030.00	$2,308.00	$1,166.00 – 4,155.00

variety of ways. The most common method of acquiring land is through transfer of ownership rights based on a monetary arrangement in the form of a downpayment and mortgage. Land for 73 percent of the single-family and 67 percent of the multifamily developments in the Dover Township sample was purchased in this manner. A straight interest note, with principal payable or renewable after a certain period of time, may replace the typical mortgage or it may be drawn up in tandem with a standard mortgage. Capital need not be invested in land at the outset of the subdivision process. However, the tract must be committed to the residential developer through a purchase option or right of assignment to guarantee the ultimate disposition of the site as planned. Twenty-two percent of the multifamily developments were proposed with land committed by option.

Land costs per unit for single-family developments in the central New Jersey coastal zone averaged $2,320.00, ranging from a low of $960.00 to a high of $3,520.00. Units in multifamily developments were assessed an average land cost of $1,280.00, with a range from $440.00 to $3,470.00. For those who held land prior to subdivision or purchased land subsequent to subdivision, these costs reflect land values updated or backdated to the commencement of the subdivision process.

Interest Costs

Interest rates on capital borrowed to finance land acquisition averaged 8 percent during the period the developers were engaged in subdivision activities. Interest charges incurred by developments are a function of the amount borrowed, rate, and duration of the loan. These charges, which reflect the duration of the subdivision process, averaged $200.00 per single-family and $50.00 per multifamily unit. The majority of both samples incurred the expense of interest charges for borrowed capital which ranged between $5.00 and $430.00 per single-family and $7.00 to $250.00 per multifamily unit. Extremely small mortgages with low interest rates account for the lower limits of these ranges. Interest payments, occurring during the period required to secure development approval, are made monthly and carried as liabilities to the conclusion of the subdivision process.

Taxes

Units in single-family development averaged real estate taxes amounting to $90.00 for the duration of the subdivision process; those in multifamily developments averaged approximately $50.00 per unit. The range was $30.00 to $170.00 for single-family and $14.00 to $160.00 for multifamily units. The variation in taxes is almost exclusively a result of the range of densities permitted. Taxes enter the cost ledger quarterly and are accumulated in the subdivision costs until the project is filed with the county recording officer.

Regulatory Costs

The cost of the coastal zone land-use regulations has been detailed in the preceding section of this chapter. Single-family developments average regulatory expenses of approximately $1,600.00 and multifamily developments about $600.00 per unit. The range in cost for single-family units is from $1,230 to $2,000, while for multifamily units it is from $450.00 to $880.00. Fees attributable to subdivision regulations require cash outlays at irregular intervals throughout the process and are entered at the point in the process where submissions are made for each regulation. The expense of each particular application is then accrued until the entire regulatory phase of the project is complete.

Carrying Costs

Of all the expenses incurred in the process of obtaining approval for a development, carrying costs are the most variable. They are calculated according to a composite rate which takes into account foregone opportunity, inflation, and risk. Every expense incurred or cash outlay made during the course of subdivision is carried until the conclusion of the process. For purposes of this study, both 15 and 20 percent[7] uncompounded annual rates were used to estimate carrying costs, thereby establishing both upper and lower estimates of the cost of inflation, risk, and opportunity.[8] At a 15 percent rate, carrying costs ranged from about $360.00 to $1,140.00 per single-family unit and $100.00 to $490.00 per multifamily unit; at a 20 percent rate the carrying costs were about $480 to $1,520.00 and $130.00 to $650.00, respectively. At a 15 percent rate, the average carrying cost is approximately $690.00 for each single-family unit and $380.00 for every multifamily unit.

Total Costs

The initial cost of the land, together with the expenses incurred as a result of interest, taxes, regulation, and carrying costs, constitute the total cost of land conversion to the developer. For single-family developments this amounts to nearly $4,900.00 per unit; for multifamily developments approximately $2,300.00. Land acquisition accounts for 47 percent of single-family development land processing costs; regulations represent 33 percent, carrying costs 14 percent, interest 4 percent, and taxes 2 percent. The figures for multifamily development processing are respectively: 55 percent (land), 26 percent (regulations), 12 percent (carrying costs), 4 percent (interest), and 2 percent (taxes).

THE STATE COASTAL ZONE PERMIT AS AN ELEMENT OF TOTAL LAND CONVERSION COSTS

The costs of the state coastal zone permit requirement as it affects the land conversion process for single-family and multifamily developments is shown in Figures 22 and 23. These costs may be compared with the costs of the standard processes as illustrated in Figures 24 and 25. A comparison of the costs associated with the standard and CAFRA-altered subdivision process in Tables 18 and 19 identifies costs associated with state coastal zone permitting and how it has modified interest, taxes, regulatory, and carrying costs.

It has been found that implementation of the CAFRA permit procedure increases the amount of time necessary to complete the traditional development process. Thus, in addition to the direct cost of application submission, the CAFRA procedure introduces an element of delay cost. The CAFRA procedure causes a two-month delay in the traditional processing of single-family developments; this delay results in an $85.00 per unit increase in costs to the developer. The multifamily site plan process (Figures 22 and 24) as altered by the CAFRA procedure is delayed by four months, thus increasing per unit costs by $92.00.

Table 20 shows CAFRA permit costs, the costs of the delay as a result of the CAFRA procedure, and the total costs associated with state permitting. The total cost for single-family developments is $135.00 per unit; for multifamily developments, the total cost is $125.00 per unit. These figures represent 7 and 12 percent of the initial land in-

FIGURE 22

THE COST OF THE CAFRA-ALTERED SUBDIVISION PROCESS

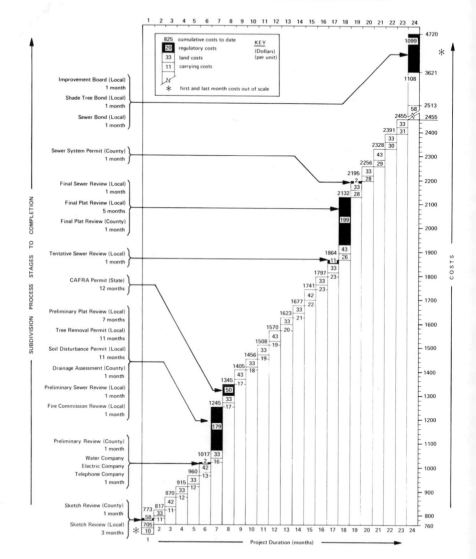

FIGURE 23

THE COST OF THE CAFRA-ALTERED SITE PLAN PROCESS

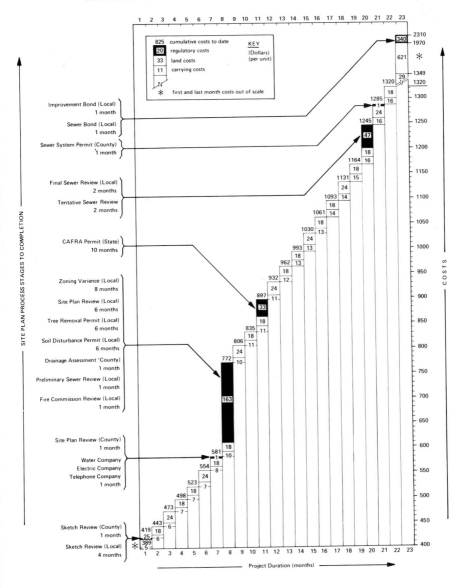

FIGURE 24

THE COST OF THE STANDARD SUBDIVISION PROCESS

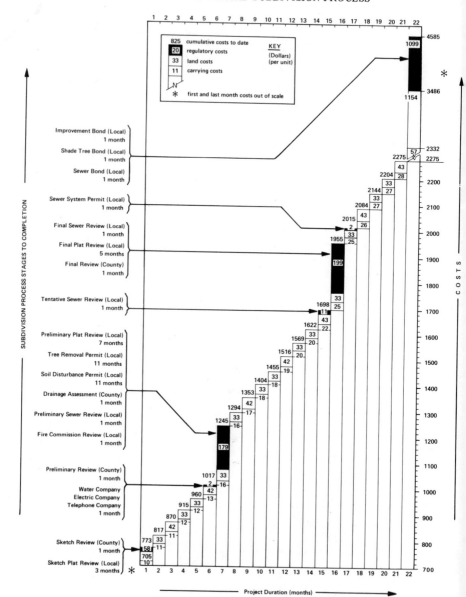

FIGURE 25

THE COST OF THE STANDARD SITE PLAN PROCESS

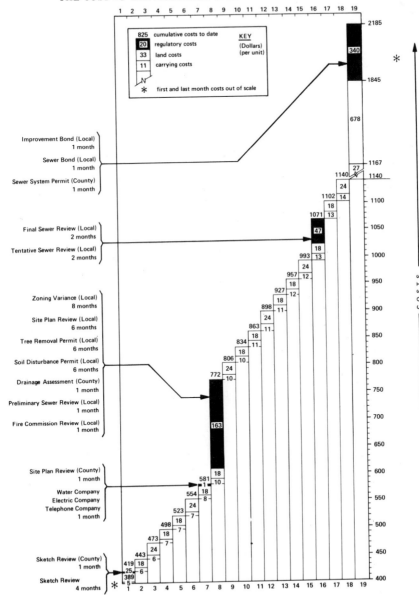

TABLE 18

COSTS INDUCED BY STATE COASTAL ZONE PERMITTING (CAFRA),
SINGLE-FAMILY DEVELOPMENTS (Dover Township, N.J., 1975)

	Standard Process	CAFRA-altered process	Cost of state permitting
Land	2319.00	2319.00	0
Interest	201.00	216.00	15.00
Taxes	65.00	71.00	6.00
Regulations	1550.00	1600.00	50.00
Carrying costs	450.00	514.00	64.00
Cost of approved land parcel	4585.00	4720.00	135.00

TABLE 19

COSTS INDUCED BY STATE COASTAL ZONE PERMITTING (CAFRA)
MULTIFAMILY DEVELOPMENTS (Dover Township, N.J., 1975)

	Standard process	CAFRA-altered process	Cost of state permitting
Land	1276.00	1276.00	0
Interest	100.00	115.00	15.00
Taxes	33.00	40.00	7.00
Regulations	576.00	609.00	33.00
Carrying costs	200.00	270.00	70.00
Cost of approved unit	2185.00	2310.00	125.00

TABLE 20

PER UNIT PERMIT AND DELAY COSTS FOR SINGLE AND
MULTIFAMILY DEVELOPMENTS *(Dover Township, N.J., 1975)*

	Cost of regulatory permit	Delay cost	Total costs
Single-family developments	$50.00	$85.00	$135.00
Multi-family developments	33.00	92.00	125.00

vestment for single-family and multifamily developments, respectively, and an additional 2 and 3 percent increase for each in the cost of land conversion.

SUMMARY

The total cost of state intervention in the land conversion process in the Dover Township, New Jersey area is represented by the CAFRA permitting procedure costs which are approximately $135.00 per unit for single-family developments and $125.00 per unit for multifamily developments. Housing costs are often estimated as a function of multiplers.[9] There are rules of thumb, for instance, which relate the cost of improved land to a residential unit's market value. These multipliers are generally accepted by appraisers, land surveyors, and market analysts.[10] All regulatory costs are included within the estimate of an improved land parcel's value prior to estimating the total structure value. These multipliers are "8" for single-family units and "6" for multifamily units. If, in fact, state regulatory costs are transmitted to structure value as local costs have been, the previously listed figures—$135 and $125—would mean that the housing consumer would have to pay an additional $1,100 for a single-family unit or $750 for a multifamily housing unit in that portion of the coastal zone subject to state regulation.

NOTES

1. Cost figures quoted in this study are in actual rather than constant dollars. Inflation is accounted for in the carrying cost calculations.
2. Muller and James, 1975, pp. 24-25.

3. No wetlands or floodplain permits were required of these developments.

4. Where required, state permits for septic systems, sewer line extensions, floodplains, and wetlands must be acquired; the costs to acquire these must be considered as additions to the figures quoted for the typical project's approval-gathering sequence prior to preliminary platting. This step of the coastal subdivision process costs $54.00 per single-family unit and $26.00 per multifamily unit; should both a special local environmental review and a state transportation permit be involved, the levy is increased to $68.00 and $34.00, respectively.

5. Should the developer fail to arrange an alternate contract, the county may also charge a drainage assessment potentially as high as $61.00 per unit depending upon a site's drainage characteristics and the project's contribution to runoff in the drainage basin.

6. Department of Environmental Protection, 1975, p.6.

7. Lindeman, 1974, pp. 45-46.

8. The 15 percent estimate of carrying costs will be used in all calculations for the remainder of the study.

9. Sternlieb, *et al.*, 1972.

10. Rahenkamp, 1975, personal communication.

Chapter 8

Conclusions and Policy Recommendations

GOVERNMENT REGULATORY ACTIVITIES
IN THE COASTAL ZONE

Many states either utilize or are preparing to utilize an interim permit-review procedure until a more comprehensive coastal zone management program can be formulated. However, a state permitting system may often duplicate regulatory procedures already existing at the local level. As a result, two separate and distinct administrative processes emerge which significantly increase the time required to process a coastal development proposal. This has obvious effects on the costs associated with such processing. The trend toward institutionalizing the state permit procedure in an operational state management program provides further incentives to develop a processing scheme that will be sensitive to multiple levels of government. At present, the absence of such sensitivity is expressed in excessively drawn out and complicated development filing procedures.

A multilayered system of land-use controls in the coastal zone is evolving—one which reflects the convergence of both planning and resource management theories. State land-use laws are emerging which not only require that governments must have a local plan before they can zone or subdivide land but also that this plan cannot conflict with the general objectives of resource management strategies at higher levels of government. The coastal zone presents a unique situation in which multiple levels of government have direct regulatory control and interact together over a common area.

THE COSTS OF STATE ENTRY AT VARIOUS
POINTS IN THE SUBDIVISION PROCESS

States which have imposed interim permitting on coastal development in addition to local subdivision regulations, have not always
chosen the same point in the permit process to exercise state review. In
New Jersey, state review currently occurs after preliminary plat submission. In other states, entry may occur after preliminary approval or
final plat approval.

The cost of state permit procedures regulating major facilities
varies according to the point at which the state chooses to enter the
local regulatory process. Figures 26/27, 28/29, and 30/31 illustrate the
costs of state permit procedures, as they occur subsequent to local preliminary plat submission, preliminary plat approval, and final plat approval, respectively for single and multifamily developments. The cost
differential according to point of entry is reproduced in Table 21. For
single-family developments, processing costs per unit increase by a
factor of "4", depending upon point of state entry. If state entry occurs simultaneously with preliminary plat submission, the state review
costs the coastal zone developer an additional $135.00; if state entry
occurs subsequent to final plat approval, the figure is $534.00. For
multifamily developments, costs can potentially double depending upon point of entry. If the state enters the regulatory process
simultaneously with submission of the site plan, state review adds
$125.00 to subdivision processing costs; if state entry occurs after all
local approvals, the additional cost amounts to $241.00. Obviously,
these differences in cost are a function of additional processing time.
State entry subsequent to preliminary plat submission is the most cost-
efficient review method, adding only two months to single-family development processing and four months to multifamily processing.
State entry subsequent to final plat approval is the least efficient
method, increasing processing time for single-family developments by
eleven months and adding nine months to the multifamily development
process.

If the state review of single-family developments could be reduced
by two months, there would be no state-induced delay of local processing. The cost of the state review could thus be reduced to $50 per unit.
Similarly, for multifamily development, if the state could reduce its review period to six months, there would be no state-induced delay

TABLE 21

*PER UNIT COST OF STATE MAJOR FACILITIES PERMITTING BY
POINT OF STATE INVOLVEMENT IN LOCAL PROCESSING
(Dover Township, N.J., 1975)*

Cost Element	Subsequent to Preliminary Plat Submission	Subsequent to Preliminary Plat Approval	Subsequent to Final Plat Approval
Single-family case			
Regulatory permit	$ 50.00	$ 50.00	$ 50.00
Delay	85.00	323.00	484.00
Total	135.00	373.00	534.00
Multifamily case			
Regulatory permit	$ 33.00	$ 33.00	$ 33.00
Delay	92.00	155.00	208.00
Total	$125.00	$188.00	$241.00

FIGURE 26

COST OF CAFRA-ALTERED SINGLE-FAMILY SUBDIVISION REVIEW PROCESS
(Point of State Entry – Subsequent to Preliminary Plat Submission)

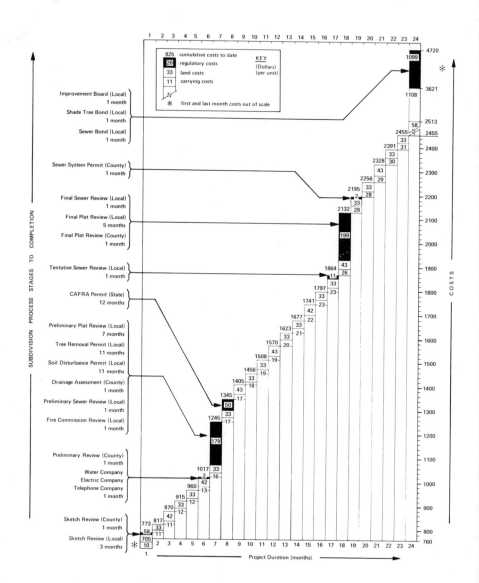

FIGURE 27

COST OF CAFRA-ALTERED MULTIFAMILY SITE PLAN REVIEW PROCESS
(Point of Entry — Subsequent to Site Plan Submission)

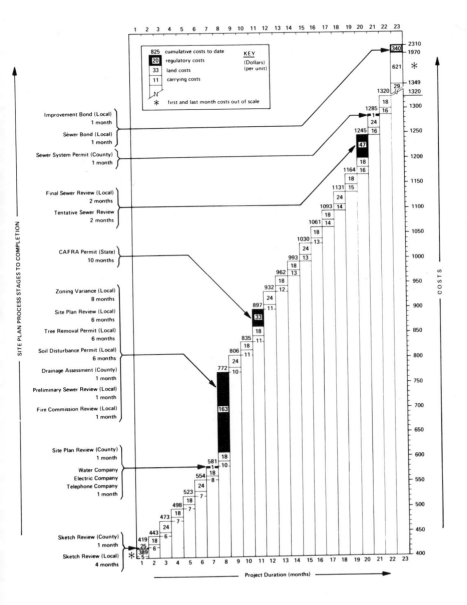

FIGURE 28

COST OF CAFRA-ALTERED SINGLE-FAMILY SUBDIVISION REVIEW PROCESS
(Point of State Entry — Subsequent to Preliminary Plat Approval)

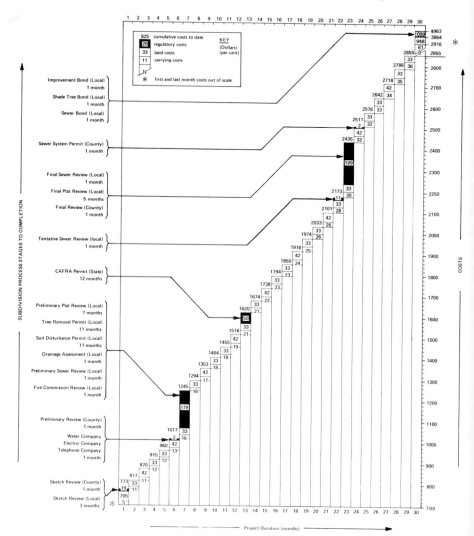

FIGURE 29

COST OF CAFRA-ALTERED MULTIFAMILY SITE PLAN REVIEW PROCESS
(Point of State Entry — Subsequent to Site Plan Approval)

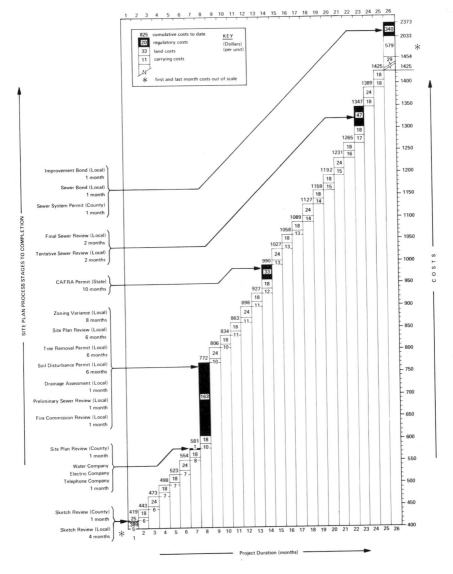

FIGURE 30

COST OF CAFRA-ALTERED SINGLE-FAMILY SUBDIVISION REVIEW PROCESS
(Point of State Entry – Subsequent to Final Plat Approval)

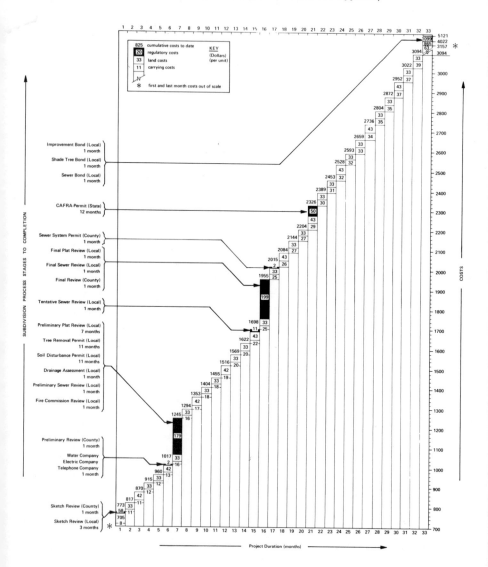

FIGURE 31

COST OF CAFRA-ALTERED MULTIFAMILY SITE PLAN REVIEW PROCESS
(Point of State Entry — Subsequent to All Local Approvals)

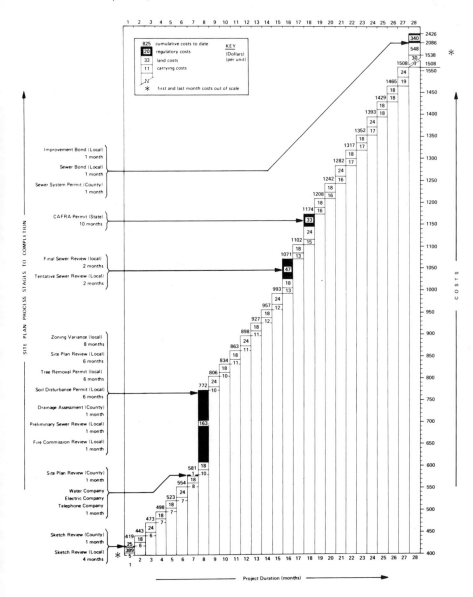

costs. This would cut the costs resulting from state review to $33.00 per unit for multifamily developments.

Up to this point, only the costs resulting from state permitting have been considered. There are also functional considerations. The sketch plat, preliminary plat, and final plat approval represent increasing degrees of finality in the development process. Basically, sketch plat approval is an agreement in concept, preliminary plat approval is an agreement on a plan for the land site, and final plat is an agreement on the most specific aspects of design. As finality increases, so, too, does cost. Regulatory costs incurred immediately prior to final plat approval, for instance, are much more severe than the costs incurred for sketch plat approval.

Since it is more costly for the developer to make changes in the development proposal during the final stages of the regulatory process, it would seem that it would be less costly to the developer if state permitting took place early in the regulatory process, before a basic plan or design agreement was negotiated between local regulatory agencies and the developer. The only valid reason for the state to delay entry would be a desire to allow unacceptable development proposals to be sifted out. This would assume that a significant number of developments that enter the sketch plat phase never receive final plat approval. However, at least for New Jersey, this assumption does not hold true. Most of the developments which receive sketch plat approval also eventually receive final plat approval. Although one out of two proposals receive some modification and one out of three have to be resubmitted, the fact remains that in excess of nine out of ten development proposals ultimately receive approval. Therefore, there would seem to be no justification for the state to delay its entry into the regulatory process, especially since such delay would add significant costs to the developer and, ultimately, to the housing consumer.

IMMINENT COASTAL ZONE REGULATORY AND COST CONSIDERATIONS

The success of the coastal zone program ultimately depends upon the management scheme developed to implement it. A whole host of considerations are incumbent upon state officials because far more is required than the mere coordination of mandated program activities and existing land use law to produce tangible results. An imminent question that must be faced by coastal states, currently immersed in program formulation, is not only what mechanisms and authority are available to regulate coastal activities, but, in addition what impact these administrative strategies will have. Programs which encourage public participation by providing a highly visible, accessible, and accountable implementing organization that is intended to protect both statewide and local interests will go a long way toward creating a climate of acceptance rather than avoidance.

An efficient multilevel governmental structure which deals equitibly with diverse situations while maintaining flexibility should also be a goal in the development of a coastal zone regulatory system. The organizational ability to implement a coastal zone program is dependent upon the establishment of intergovernmental cooperation and clearly defined operating mandates at all levels of government. The fact that each state is constrained to varying degrees by a political climate favoring preservation of local land-use perogatives precludes many of the alternative management organizations suggested in the federal guidelines for the Coastal Zone Management Act of 1972. Whatever management apparatus is adopted—whether it be entirely local government regulation, local regulation with state review of plans, local regulation with state permitting authority over critical areas and particular land uses, or state regulation with minimal local participation—the system will have to contend with the dilemma of delegating authority. Linking the level of government commensurate with the scope of the proposed activity's impact has been suggested as a possible solution to such a dilemma; however, the multilevel organization necessary to implement such a solution has been established in only a few coastal states with the majority still maneuvering for such a regulatory system.

A pertinent issue in the implementation of a coastal zone program is the selection of the appropriate type of administrative agency—superagency, special agency, or coordinating agency. For example, in a permit system relying heavily upon referrals for review and comment, a superagency, which provides most of the review capability within a single department, allows for more timely processing of development applications than a coordinating agency forced to circulate paperwork among several agencies. Special agencies may be better suited to the task of local plan review, and the coordinating agency may be most efficient in bridging the gap between the state and the locality in a local-oriented management strategy.

Several techniques for controlling land use are available for use by coastal states with regulatory authority. Special state plans have traditionally been employed to cope with specific problems. Model ordinances or development codes have been promulgated for adoption by lower levels of government exercising regulatory authority. More recent regulatory schemes have relied upon protective orders authorized through special legislation and administered via permitting procedures. An environmental impact review has often been incorporated into these permitting procedures in response to the National Environmental Protection Act (NEPA). Nearly every coastal state has some form of permit procedure designed to control the use of critical areas, certain types of pollution, and/or specific land uses. (See Table 6.)

To date, most coastal states have not officially adopted either a model ordinance or specific enabling legislation for the environmental impact statement (EIS) which often accompanies a state's permitting procedure. In developing a model EIS for the coastal zone, the state must satisfy both the U.S. Department of Commerce, which is directly responsible for coastal zone activities, and the U.S. Department of Housing and Urban Development, which is the catalyst for most major housing and public works projects. The EIS must also be acceptable to all local, regional, or federal authorities which have jurisdiction in the coastal zone. In this regard, a developer in the coastal area who desires to offer FHA mortgages to consumers, should only be required to file one EIS which would simultaneously meet local, state, HUD, and NOAA requirements.

In addition to the issues surrounding selection of an EIS format and traditional forms of regulations, states are faced with the task of wisely utilizing existing coastal resources by means of supplemental regulatory techniques such as revised subdivision laws, dedication and in-lieu fees, density bonuses, lot consolidation requirements, and transfer of development rights. Beyond the establishment of an organizational structure and compatible management strategy which reflect lines of governmental authority within the state, the proper mix of supplemental regulations is a prime determinant of how well the state influences activities which are permitted to locate in the coastal zone. Coastal states must decide the basic issue of whether to combine prohibitive regulation with promotional techniques to further the scope of their coastal zone management programs.

Any attempt to foster equity and efficiency in the implementation of state coastal zone management strategies must ultimately address the cost of carrying out that strategy. Agency administrative expenses and land acquisition-development costs are but one side of the cost ledger in a cost/benefit analysis of coastal zone management. The coastal zone program's impact on private sector costs, which are ultimately borne by the consumer, have become a major concern in coastal states administering interim controls. It may be anticipated that almost every coastal state will be required to assess the impact of both its chosen coastal zone management plan and the administrative policies utilized to implement it. Insight derived from these assessments, if they are conducted during the state's program formulation, should prove useful in the selection of an appropriate organizational structure and complementing regulations. In sum, it is incumbent upon states to realize that coastal zone management's impact on private costs is just as relevant in program development as its effect on public costs. This consideration is particularly pertinent in view of many states' emphasis on public participation and an acknowledged need to understand the source of so much development activity in the coastal zone, the real estate market.

This study has examined the evolution of a multilevel regulatory system in a particular coastal state, New Jersey. The management apparatus in this state combines local regulation with state permitting authority over critical areas and particular land uses. In New Jersey, major facilities permitting is administered by what may be considered a superagency, utilizing a procedure which includes numerous review and comment referrals. New Jersey's permit, CAFRA, does incorporate an EIS requirement; however, standardization of the format has not been achieved. A prohibitive management philosphy is apparent, particularly during the interim period preceding formulation of the coastal zone program. The New Jersey experience provides an opportunity to assess the direct private sector costs of various administrative policies, and to document the changes in the rather standard subdivision process brought about by initiation of state permitting authority. The multilevel regulatory system that has emerged is believed to preface a national trend toward this type of land use control, particularly in the coastal zone.

It has been the objective of this study to demonstrate the cost of environmental protection for housing in one specific area, the coastal zone. These costs have been shown to escalate as a function of administrative procedures and policies. Therefore, it is of utmost importance that the various levels of government involved in regulating land use in the coastal zone coordinate their efforts into sound and efficient procedures. Hopefully, this research will contribute to that goal.

Bibliography

PROFESSIONAL REFERENCES:

Alexander, Larry, *et al:*, *Remote Sensing Environmental and Geotechnical Applications—The State of the Art*, Engineering Bulletin No. 45 (Los Angeles: Dames & Moore, August 1974).

Armstrong, John, *et al.*, *Coastal Zone Managment: The Process of Program Development* (Sandwich, Mass. Coastal Zone Management Institute, November 1974).

Bardin, David J., "Coastal Zone Management in New Jersey Today: From Action and Planning to More Action." A paper presented at the *Third Annual National Coastal Zone Management Conference* (Asilomar, Calif.: Office of Coastal Zone Management, NOAA, U.S. Department of Commerce, May 1975).

Bartelli, L.J., Klingebiel, A.A., Baird, J.V., and Heddleson, M.R., editors, *Soil Surveys and Land Use Planning* (Madison, Wis.: Soil Science Society of America and American Society of Agronomy, 1966).

Battelle Columbus Laboratories, *Environmental Evaluation System for Water Resource Planning* (Columbus, Ohio: 1972).

Baum, Alvin H. and associates, *Economic Impacts of the Proposed Coastal Plan—A First Report and Further Proposals* (San Francisco, Calif.: The Joint Rules Committee of the California Legislature, October 1975).

Beller, William S., "Ocean Islands—Considerations for their Coastal Zone Management," *Coastal Zone Management Journal*, Vol. I, No., 1, Fall 1973.

Bennett, John E., "Managing California's Coastal Zone Resource," *Shore and Beach*, Vol. XL, No. 2, October 1972.

Bergman, Edward M., "Development Controls & Housing Costs: A Policy Guide to Research," *Management & Control of Growth* (Washington, D.C.: Urban Land Institute, 1975) Vol. III, pp. 527-536.

Bernstein, Harry E. and Bernstein, Daniel S., *Legal Aspects of Planning and Zoning* (New Brunswick, N.J.: Bureau of Government Research and University Extension Division, Rutgers University March 1971).

Berry, Brian J.L. and Bednarz, Robert S., "A Hedonic Model of Prices and Assessments for Single-Family Homes: Does the Assessor Follow the Market or the Market Follow the Assessor?" *Land Economics* (Madison, Wis.: University of Wisconsin Press), Vol. LI, No. 1, February 1975.

Beuscher, J.H., *Land Use Controls—Cases and Materials* (Madison, Wis.: University of Wisconsin Press, 1966).

Biggs, John A., *Application for Federal Grant under Section 305 of the Coastal Zone Management Act of 1972* (Olympia, Wash.: Washington Department of Ecology, May 1974).

Bishop, A.B., *et al.*, *Carrying Capacity in Regional Environmental Management* (Washington, D.C.: U.S. Environmental Protection Agency, February, 1974).

Blomenfeld, Charles R., "State Coastal Zone Programs: Property Owners Beware," *Environmental Comment* (Washington, D.C.: Urban Land Institute), April 1975.

Board of Chosen Freeholders, *Subdivision Review and Site Plan*

Review Resolutions (Toms River, N.J.: Ocean County Board of Chosen Freeholders, June 1970).

Bosselman, Fred and Callies, David, *The Quiet Revolution in Land Use Control* (Washington, D.C.: Council on Environmental Quality, 1971).

Bosselman, Fred, Callies, David, and Banta, John, *The Taking Issue* (Washington, D.C.: Council on Environmental Quality, 1973).

Brennan, William J., editor, *Commerce News* (Washington, D.C.: U.S. Department of Commerce), 1974-1975.

Bressan, Davis J., *et al.*, *Narragansett Marine Bibliography* (Kingston, R.I.: Marine Resources Program, University of Rhode Island, 1968).

Brewer, William C., Jr., "The Concept of State and Local Relations Under the CZMA," *William and Mary Law Review* (Williamsburg, Va.: The Marshall-Wythe School of Law, College of William and Mary), Vol. XVI, No. 4, Summer 1975.

Buckwald, George H., chairman, *Ocean County Planning Board Annual Report, 1973* (Toms River, N.J.: Ocean County Planning Board, 1973).

Burchell, Robert W. and Listokin, David, editors, *Future Land Use* (New Brunswick, N.J.: Center for Urban Policy Research, Rutgers University, 1975a).

Burchell, Robert W. and Listokin, David, *The Environmental Impact Handbook* (New Brunswick, N.J.: Center for Urban Policy Research, Rutgers University, 1975b).

Burgweger, Francis J., Jr., "The California Coastal Zone Conservation Act of 1972: A Sampling of Developers' Problems," *Environmental Comment* (Washington, D.C.: Urban Land Institute), April 1975.

Cameron, Francis X., "NEPA and the CZMA: The Environmental Impact Statement and Section 306 Guidelines," *William and Mary Law Review* (Williamsburg, Va.: The Marshall-Wythe School of Law, College of William and Mary), Vol. XVI, No. 4, Summer 1975.

California Coastal Zone Conservation Commission, *Preliminary Coastal Plan* (San Francisco, Calif.: State of California, March 1975).

Chapin, F. Stuart, Jr., *Urban Land Use Planning* (Chicago, Ill.: University of Illinois Press, 1972).

Chavooshian, B. Budd and Norman, Thomas, *Transfer of Development Rights: A New Concept in Land Use Management* (New Brunswick, N.J.: Rutgers University, 1974).

Chavooshian, B. Budd, Nieswand, George, and Norman, Thomas *Growth-Managment Program*, Leaflet 503 (New Brunswick N.J.: Cooperative Extension Service, Rutgers University, 1974).

Chief Statistician's Office, *Population Projections for New Jersey 1970-2000* (Newark, N.J.: New Jersey Bell Telephone Company, June 1972).

Clark, John, *Coastal Ecosystems* (Washington, D.C.: The Conservation Foundation, 1974).

Clawson, Marion, *Suburban Land Conversion in the United States* (Baltimore, Md.: The Johns Hopkins University Press, 1971).

Coastal Area Review Board, "Decision on Appeal of CAFRA Application CA 73-003: Lehigh Construction Company." Department of Environmental Protection CAFRA Appeal No. 1, January 3, 1975.

Coastal Coordinating Council, *Unofficial Composite of General Permitting Procedures for Coastal Zone Activities in Florida* (Tallahassee: Florida Department of Natural Resources, June 1971).

Coastal Coordinating Council, *Marine Environmental Studies of Florida's Gulf Coast: Summary and Selected Bibliography*

(Tallahassee: Florida Department of Natural Resources, 1973a).

Coastal Coordinating Council, *Clearwater Coastal Zone Management Plan* (Tallahassee: Florida Department of Natural Resources, 1973b).

Coastal Coordinating Council, *Statistical Inventory of Key Biophysical Elements in Florida's Coastal Zone* (Tallahassee: Florida Department of Natural Resources, 1973c).

Coastal Coordinating Council, *Florida Coastal Zone Management Atlas* (Tallahassee: Florida Department of Natural Resources, 1973d).

Coastal Coordinating Council, *Recommendations for Development Activities in Florida's Coastal Zone* (Tallahassee: Florida Department of Natural Resources, 1973e).

Coastal Coordinating Council, *Florida Keys Coastal Management Study* (Tallahassee: Florida Department of Natural Resources, June 1974).

Coastal Plains Center for Marine Development Services, *The Marine Newsletter* (Wilmington, N.C.) 1970-1975.

Coastal Plains Center for Marine Development Services, *Directory of Facilities* (Wilmington, N.C.: March 1971).

Coastal Plains Center for Marine Development Services, *Proceedings of Seminar on Planning and Engineering in the Coastal Zone*, Seminar Series No. 2, Charleston, N.C.: 1972).

Coastal Plains Center for Marine Development Services, *A Directory of Bibliographies Relevant to the Environment and Activities of the Coastal Plains Region* (Wilmington, N.C.: 1972).

Coastal Zone Management Program, *Proceedings: Mid-Atlantic States Quarterly Coastal Zone Management Conference* (Sandy Hook, N.J.: New Jersey Department of Environmental Protection, October 1975).

Commission on Marine Science, Engineering, and Resources, *Our Nation and the Sea* (Washington, D.C.: U.S. Government Printing Office, 1969).

Connecticut Department of Environmental Protection, *Citizen's Bulletin*, Vol. II, No. 1, October 1974.

Connecticut Department of Environmental Protection, *Citizen's Bulletin*, Vol. II, No. 2, November 1974.

Council of State Governments, *A Legislator's Guide to Land Management* (Lexington, Ky.: The Council of State Governments, 1974).

Curtis, Virginia, editor, *Land Use and the Environment* (Chicago, Ill.: American Society of Planning Officials, 1973).

Daughterty, Richard, *Science in Geography, Part 2. Data Collection* (New York: Oxford University Press, 1974).

Davidoff, Paul, "Advocacy and Pluralism in Planning," *Journal of the American Institute of Planners*, Vol. 1, No. 4, November 1965.

Davis, Peter, *Science in Geography, Part 3. Data Description and Presentation* (New York: Oxford University Press, 1974).

Delaware River and Bay Marine Council, *Final Report* (Trenton: N.J. Department of Environmental Protection, December 1972).

Delaware State Planning Office, *Proceedings of First Mid-atlantic States Coastal Zone Management Workshop* (Dover: Delaware State Executive Department, August 1974).

Devanney, J.W., *et al.*, *Economic Factors in the Development of a Coastal Zone* (Cambridge, Mass.: Massachusetts Institute of Technology, November 1970).

Douglas, Peter M., "Coastal Zone Management—A New Approach in California," *Coastal Zone Management Journal,* Vol. 1, No. 1, Fall 1973.

Dover Sewerage Authority, *Rules and Regulations* (Toms River, N.J.: Charles J. Kupper, Inc., 1971).

Dover Township Committee, *Code of the Township of Dover, New Jersey* (Toms River, N.J.: Township of Dover) as amended.

Dover Township Planning Board, *Dover Township Master Plan* (Toms River, N.J.: Township of Dover, 1972).

Downs, Anthony and Lachman, M. Leanne, "The Current Climate for Real Estate Investment and Development," *Real Estate Review* (New York, N.Y.: The Real Estate Institute of New York University) Vol. VI, No. 1, Spring 1974.

Dresdner, Allan, *Coastal Zone Management* (Crawford, N.J.: Dames & Moore, 1974).

Duxbury Planning Board, *Duxbury Comprehensive Plan Statement* (Duxbury, Mass.: Rahenkamp, Sachs, Wells and Associates, 1973).

Ellis, Robert H., "Coastal Zone Management System: A Combination of Tools," *Tools for Coastal Zone Management* (Washington, D.C.: Marine Technology Society) February 1972, pp. 95-112.

Environmental Quality Committee, *Shorelines Management: The Washington Experience* (Seattle: Washington State Sea Grant Program, 1972).

Fallows, James M., *The Water Lords* (New York: Grossman Publishers, 1971).

Fidelity Union Trust Company, *Expanded Payment Table for Monthly Mortgage Loans* (Boston: Financial Publishing Company, 1969).

Fischer, Joseph A. and Fox, Fred L., *et al., Siting Considerations for Offshore Nuclear Power Plants,* Engineering Bulletin 42, (Los Angeles: Dames & Moore, September 1973).

Forste, Robert H., editor, *Proceedings: The New England Coastal Zone Management Conference, April 28-29, 1970* (Durham, N.H.: The New England Center for Continuing Education, December 1970).

Frank, Michael, "Performance Zoning Aids Rational Development," *Environmental Action Bulletin,* May 17, 1975.

Gansberg, Martin "Jersey Weighs Land-Use Shift," *The New York Times,* July 13, 1975.

Gardner, Richard B., "Policy Alternatives," *Managing Our Coastal Zone: Proceedings of a Conference on Coastal Zone Management* (Albany, N.Y.: New York State Sea Grant Program 1973).

Goodman, William I. and Freund, Eric C., *Principles and Practice of Urban Planning* (Washington, D.C.: International City Managers Association, 1968).

Governor's Task Force on Marine and Coastal Affairs, *The Coastal Zone of Delaware* (Newark, Del.: College of Marine Studies, University of Delaware, July 1972).

Grant, Malcolm J., *Rhode Island's Ocean Sands: Management Guidelines for Sand and Gravel Extraction in State Waters,* Marine Technical Report No. 10 (Kingston, R.I.: Coastal Resources Center, University of Rhode Island, 1973).

Grant, Malcolm J., *Perspectives on Coastal Management: Marine Trades and the Coastal Crisis,* Marine Bulletin Series No. 18 (Kingston, R.I.: The Coastal Resources Center, University of Rhode Island, 1974).

Greenberg, Michael R. and Hordon, Robert M., "Environmental

Impact Statements: Some Annoying Questions," *AIP Journal,* May 1974.

Haskell, Elizabeth H. and Price, Victoria S., *State Environmental Management* (New York: Praeger Publishers, 1973).

Heller, Alfred, editor, *The California Tomorrow Plan* (Los Altos, Calif.: William Kaufmann, Inc., 1972).

Hershman, Marc J., "Achieving Federal-State Coordination in Coastal Resources Management," *William and Mary Law Review* (Williamsburg, Va.: The Marshall-Wythe School of Law, College of William and Mary), Vol. XVI, No. 4, Summer 1975.

Hershman, Marc J., editor, *Coastal Zone Management Journal* (New York: Crane, Russak & Company, Inc., 1973-74).

Hildreth, Richard G., "Coastal Land Use Control in Sweden," *Coastal Zone Management Journal,* **Vol. 2, No. 1, 1975.**

Hite, James C. and Stepp, James M., editors, *Coastal Zone Resource Management* (New York: Praeger Publishers, 1971).

Hollings, Ernest F., "Congress and Coastal Zone Management," *Coastal Zone Management Journal* (New York: Crane, Russak & Co., Inc.), Vol. 1, No. 1, Fall 1973.

Institute of Environmental Studies, *Environmental Factors Which Shape Local Planning* (New Brunswick, N.J.: Rutgers University, 1975).

Interdepartmental Committee for State Planning, *Setting for the New Jersey State Development Plan* (Trenton: State of New Jersey, April 1966).

Juneja, Narendra, *Medford* (Philadelphia: Pa.: Center for Ecological Research in Planning and Design, University of Pennsylvania, 1974).

Kaiser, Edward J., *et al., Promoting Environmental Quality Through Urban Planning and Controls* (Washington, D.C.: Office of Research and Development, U.S. Environmental Protection Agency, February 1974).

Kelly, Eric D., *The Legal Context for Impact Zoning in New Jersey* (Philadelphia, Pa.: Rahenkamp, Sachs, Wells, and Associates, 1974).

Kendrick, Ned, Planning in the Coastal Zone, (Cambridge, Mass.: Harvard University, unpublished manuscript, 1974).

Kenny, Kenneth B., *The Residential Land Developer and His Land Purchase Decision* Environmental Policies and Urban Development Thesis No. 16 (Chapel Hill, N.C.: Center for Urban and Regional Studies, University of North Carolina, 1972).

Kesler, Nancy, "Plan for Managing Coast Zone Sought," *The Morning News* (Dover, Delaware), June 27, 1974.

Ketchum, Bostwick H., *The Water's Edge: Critical Problems of the Coastal Zone* (Cambridge, Mass.: The MIT Press, 1972).

Koppelman, Lee E., *Integration of Coastal Zone Science and Regional Planning* (New York: Praeger Publishers, 1974).

Koppelman, Lee E., "Models for Implementing the CZMA's Concept of State-Local Relations," *William and Mary Law Review* (Williamsburg, Va.: The Marshall-Wythe School of Law, College of William and Mary), Vol. XVI, No. 4, Summer 1975.

Knecht, Robert W., "Coastal Zone Management—A Federal Perspective," *Coastal Zone Management Journal,* Vol. I, No. 1, Fall 1973.

Kruger, Robert B., "Coastal Zone Management: The California Experience," *Shore and Beach,* Vol. XL, No. 2, October 1972.

Laird, Beverly L., *Documents Related to Management of the*

Coastal Zone: An Annotated Bibliography (Gloucester Point, Va.: Virginia Institute of Marine Science, July 1973).

Lamb, Charles M., *Land Use Politics and Law in the 1970's,* Monograph 28 (Washington, D.C.: George Washington University, January 1975).

Lauf, Ted, "Shoreland Regulation in Wisconsin," *Coastal Zone Management Journal,* Vol. 2, No. 1, 1975.

Levin, Melvin R., Rose, Jerome G., and Slavet, Joseph S., *New Approaches to State Land-Use Policies* (Lexington, Mass.: D.C. Heath and Company, 1974).

Lindeman, J. Bruce, "Is the Land Boom Coming to an End?" *Real Estate Review,* Vol. 4, No. 3, Fall 1974.

Listokin, David, editor, *Land Use Controls: Present Problems and Future Reform* (New Brunswick, N.J.: Center for Urban Policy Research, Rutgers University, 1974).

Louisiana Advisory Commission on Coastal and Marine Resources, *Louisiana Government and the Coastal Zone—1972* (Baton Rouge, La.: Law Center, Louisiana State University, March 1972).

Louisiana Advisory Commission on Coastal and Marine Resources, *Wetlands '73: Toward Coastal Zone Management in Louisiana* (Baton Rouge, La.: Law Center, Louisiana State University, March 1973).

Lubell, Harold A., "Environmental Legislation and Real Estate," *Real Estate Review* (New York: The Real Estate Institute of New York University), Vol. IV, No. 1, Spring 1974.

Lynch, Kevin, *Site Planning* (Cambridge, Mass.: The MIT Press, 1971).

Lynch, M.P., Laird, B.L., and Smolen, T.F., *Marine and Estuarine Sanctuaries: Proceedings of the National Workshop on*

Sanctuaries, 28-30 November, 1973, Washington, D.C., Special scientific report no. 70 (Glouster Point, Va.: Virginia Institute of Marine Science, February 1974).

Mandelker, Daniel R. and Montgomery, Roger, *Housing in America: Problems and Perspectives* (New York: The Bobbs-Merrill Company, Inc., 1973).

Marine Sciences Center, *Review of Selected New Jersey Coastal Area Legislation* (New Brunswick, N.J.: Rutgers University, 1975).

Marine Technology Society, *Tools for Coastal Zone Management* (Washington, D.C.: February, 1972).

Marsh, Lindell L., "Regulation, Taking and Planning in The California Coastal Zone," *Proceedings: Coastal Zone Management and the Western States Future* (Newport Beach, Calif.: Marine Technology Society), December 1973).

McCandless, Thomas C., Analysis and Correlation of Sale Data for Green Island (unpublished manuscript, 1967).

McDonough, William R., "Buyers, Builders, and Instability in Single-Family Housing Construction," *Journal of Economics and Business* (Philadelphia, Pa.: Temple University, School of Business Administration) Vol. 27, No. 2, Winter 1975.

McGrath, Dorn C., Jr., "Implementing National Policies: Bigger Carrots, Bigger Sticks," *Land-Use Policies* (Chicago, Ill.: American Society of Planning Officials, 1970), pp. 29-37.

McHarg, Ian L., *Design with Nature* (Garden City, N.Y.: The Natural History Press, 1969).

McHugh, J.L., "Are Estuaries Necessary," *Commercial Fish Review*, Vol. 30, No. 11, 1968.

Merselis, William B., editor, *Proceedings Coastal Zone Management and The Western States Future* (Newport Beach, Calif.: Marine

Technology Society, Los Angeles Region Section, December 1973).

Meta Systems, Inc., *An Operational Framework for Coastal Zone Management Planning* (Washington, D.C.: Office of Research and Technology, U.S. Department of Interior, January 1975).

Meyerson, Martin, "The Do-Gooders and the Good-Doers: Business Leadership and the Revival of Cities," *The Tobe Lectures in Retail Distribution, 1959-1960* (Boston, Mass.: Division of Research, Harvard Business School, 1960).

Middlesex County Planning Board, *Site Plan Review Resolution* (Middlesex County, N.J.: June 1974a).

Middlesex County Planning Board, *Land Subdivision Resolution* (Middlesex County, N.J.: June 1974b).

Miller, Nathan J., "Selling the Deal to the Landowner," *Real Estate Review*, Vol. 4, No. 3, Fall 1974.

Miller, William R. and Whitney, Scott C., "Data Management in Coastal Zone Planning," *William and Mary Law Review* (Williamsburg, Va.: The Marshall-Wythe School of Law, College of William and Mary), Vol. XVI, No. 4, Summer 1975.

Miloy, Leatha F., "Coastal and Marine Information Dissemination Programs," *Coastal Zone Management Journal*, Vol. I, No. 2, Winter 1974.

Mitchell, Colin, *Terrain Evaluation* (London: Longman, Inc., 1973).

Mitchell, James K., "Coastal Management from a New Jersey Perspective." A paper delivered at the 141st Annual Meeting of the American Association for the Advancement of Sciences, New York, January 26-31, 1975.

Moore, J. Jamison, "Land Use Allocation and Coastal Zone Management," *Shore and Beach*, Vol. XL, No. 2, October 1972.

Moskowitz, Harvey S., *The Land Subdivision Ordinance of the Township of Mill Hill* (Mill Hill, N.J.: Mill Hill Township, 1974).

Muller, Thomas and James, Franklin J., "Environmental Impact Evaluation and Housing Costs." A paper delivered at the Annual Meeting of the American Real Estate and Urban Economics Association, Washington, D.C., May 29, 1975.

National Commission on Urban Problems (Douglas Commission), *Building the American City* (Washington, D.C.: 1968).

Neuschatz, Alan, *Managing the Environment* (Washington, D.C.: Washington Environmental Research Center, 1973).

New Jersey Bureau of Marine Lands Management, *Procedural Rules for the Administration of the Coastal Area Facility Review Act* (Trenton: New Jersey Department of Environmental Protection, 1974).

New Jersey Bureau of Navigation, *Riparian Rights* (Trenton: New Jersey Department of Conservation and Economic Development, 1972).

New Jersey Department of Environmental Protection, *Draft CAFRA Rules and Regulations* (Trenton, N.J.: October 31, 1975).

New Jersey Department of Environmental Protection, "Department Plan Fiscal Year 1973-1974," *Let's Protect Our Earth,* (Trenton, N.J.: 1973).

New Jersey Department of Labor and Industry, *Industrial Projections to 1980: New Jersey and Labor Market Areas* (Trenton, N.J.: November 1973).

New Jersey Division of Local Government Services, *Planning, Zoning, Environmental and Related Enabling Legislation* (Trenton: New Jersey, Department of Community Affairs, August 1974).

New Jersey Division of Local Government Services, *Planning and Zoning Inter-Agency Referral Requirements* (Trenton: New Jersey Department of Community Affairs, January 1974).

New Jersey Division of State and Regional Planning, *Administrative Guide to Subdivision Regulations* (Trenton: New Jersey Department of Community Affairs, 1969).

New Jersey Division of State and Regional Planning, *Another Way: Clustering Planned Unit Developments, New Communities* (Trenton: New Jersey Department of Community Affairs, 1974).

New Jersey Division of State and Regional Planning, *Soils in Relation to Land Use in New Jersey* (Trenton: New Jersey Department of Community Affairs, December 1966).

New Jersey Division of Water Resources, *Proposed State Land Use Regulations for Floodways* (Trenton: New Jersey Department of Environmental Protection, September 1974).

New Jersey Senate, "Ninety Day Bill," Senate No. 3088, February 27, 1975.

New York State Sea Grant Program, *Managing Our Coastal Zone: Proceedings of a Conference on Coastal Zone Management* (Albany, N.Y.: February, 1973).

Nieswand, George, Stillman, Calvin, and Esser, Tony, *Inventory of Estuarine Site Development Lagoon Systems: New Jersey Shore* (Water Resources Research Institute, Rutgers University, 1972).

Nieswand, George, Stillman, Calvin and Esser, Tony, *Survey of Estuarine Site Development Lagoon Homeowners Ocean County, New Jersey* (Water Resources Research Institute, Rutgers University, 1973).

Noble, Jack, "The Zone Busters Are Coming," *Land-Use Policies* (Chicago, Ill.: American Society of Planning Officials, 1970).

Nochimson, David, "How the Land Packager Makes His Deal," *Real Estate Review,* Vol. 4, No. 3, Fall 1974.

Norman, Thomas, editor, *New Jersey Trends* (New Brunswick, N.J.: Institute of Environmental Studies, Rutgers University, 1974).

Ocean County Planning Board, *Ocean County Population* (Toms River, N.J.: County of Ocean, January 1972).

Odell, Rice, "Carrying Capacity Analysis: Useful But Limited," *Management and Control of Growth* (Washington, D.C.: The Urban Land Institute, 1975).

Odum, William E. and Skjeik, Stephen, "The Issue of Wetlands Preservation and Management: A Second View," *Coastal Zone Management Journal,* Vol. I, No. 2, Winter 1974.

Office of Coastal Zone Management, *State Coastal Zone Management Activities* (Washington, D.C.: NOAA, Department of Commerce, October 1974).

Office of Environmental Analysis, *Application for Coastal Zone Management Program Development Grant* (Trenton: New Jersey Department of Environmental Protection, May 1974).

Office of Environmental Analysis, *Summary Report of New Jersey Coastal Zone Management Planning Program* (Trenton: New Jersey Department of Environmental Protection, February 1975).

O'Riordan, T., *Perspectives on Resource Management* (London: Pion Limited, 1971).

Oross, Eugene E., Associates, *Master Plan Report 5—Land Use Study* (Toms River, N.J.: County of Ocean, June 1973).

Oross, Eugene E., Associates, *Master Plan Report 8—Economic Development Analysis* (Toms River, N.J.: County of Ocean, June 1974a).

Oross, Eugene E., Assoc., *Master Plan Report 9—Community Facilities and Services* (Toms River, N.J.: County of Ocean, June 1974b).

Oross, Eugene E., Assoc., *Master Plan Report 10—Housing Resource and Need Analysis* (Toms River, N.J.: County of Ocean, June 1974c).

Owen, Samuel P., "A State With Growing Pains," *Land Use Policies* (Chicago, Ill.: American Society of Planning Officials, 1970), pp. 59-64.

Parke, John R., *Soils in Relation to Land Use in New Jersey* (Trenton: New Jersey Division of State and Regional Planning, Department of Conservation and Economic Development, December 1966).

Peerey, Michael R., "Balancing Equities in the Coastal Zone," *Proceedings: Coastal Zone Management and the Western States Future* (Newport Beach, Calif.: Marine Technology Society, December 1973).

Perry, Robert M., editor, *Planning and Engineering in the Marine Environments*, Engineering Bulletin No. 44 (Los Angeles, Calif.: Dames & Moore, March 1974).

Public Law 92-583, *Coastal Zone Management Act of 1972* (Washington, D.C.: 92nd Congress, S. 3507), October 27, 1972.

Public Law, 1973, Chapter 185, *Coastal Area Facility Review Act,* (Trenton: Senate and General Assembly, State of New Jersey), June 20, 1973.

Rahenkamp, John, *Fair Share Housing: A Logical Tool for Managed Growth* (Philadelphia, Pa.: Rahenkamp, Sachs, Wells, and Associates, 1974).

Rahenkamp, Sachs, Wells, and Associates, *Duxbury-North Hills Review* (Philadelphia, Pa.: 1974).

Real Estate Research Corporation, *The Costs of Sprawl—Detailed Cost Analysis* (Washington, D.C.: Council on Environmental Quality, April 1974).

Real Estate Research Corporation, *The Costs of Sprawl—Literature Review and Bibliography* (Washington, D.C.: Council on Environmental Quality, April 1974).

Reilly, William, *The Use of Land* (New York: Thomas Y. Crowell Co., 1973).

Richardson, Dan, *The Impact of CAFRA on the Non-Regulated Coastal Zone* (New Brunswick, N.J.: Marine Sciences Center, Rutgers University, October 1975).

Richardson, Dan, Zoning-Land Use Comparison (unpublished manuscript, May 1972).

Richardson, Dan, Micromodel Analysis of Zoning Effectiveness and Its Relation to Real Estate Market Value Trends (unpublished manuscript, May 1974).

Ring, Alfred A., *Real Estate Principles and Practices* (Englewood Cliffs, N.J.: Prentice-Hall, Inc., 1972).

Rogal, Brian, "Subdivision Improvement Guarantees," *Planning Advisory Service,* No. 298 (Chicago, Ill.: American Society of Planning Officials, January 1974).

Rose, Jerome G., *The Legal Advisor on Home Ownership* (Boston, Mass.: Little, Brown and Company, 1964).

Rose, Jerome G., *The Transfer of Development Rights: A New Technique of Land Use Regulation* (New Brunswick, N.J.: Center for Urban Policy Research, Rutgers University, 1975).

Rosentraub, Mark S. and Warren, Robert, Coastal Policy Development and Self-Evaluating Agencies: Information Utilization and the South Coast Regional Commission (School of Planning and Urban Studies, University of Southern California, unpublished manuscript, April 1975).

Runyan, Richard P. and Haber, Audrey, *Fundamentals of Behavioral Statistics* (Reading, Mass.: Addison-Wesley Publishing Company, 1967).

Russell, Clifford S. and Kneese, Allen V., "Establishing the Scientific, Technical, and Economic Basis for Coastal Zone Management," *Coastal Zone Management Journal,* Vol. I, No. 1, Fall 1973.

Sagalyn, Lynne B. and Sternlieb, George, *Zoning and Housing Costs* (New Brunswick, N.J.: Center for Urban Policy Research Rutgers University, 1973).

Schmid, A. Allan, "Tax Policy and Land Use Guidance Techniques," *Land-Use Policies* (Chicago, Ill.: American Society of Planning Officials, 1970), pp. 19-20.

Schmidt, R.A., "Needed-A Coastwise Comprehensive Program for the Development of Estuaries," *American Fisheries Society* Special Publication 3, pp. 50-58.

Schneider, Lee D., *New Jersey Land-Use Planning Techniques and Legislation* (New Brunswick, N.J.: New Jersey Agricultural Experiment Station, July 1972).

Schnidman, Frank and Kendall, Susan, "Coastal Zone Management: An Overview," *Environmental Comment* (Washington, D.C.: Urban Land Institute, April 1975).

Schwaderer, Roseann, editor, *Coastal Zone Management Newsletter* (Washington, D.C: Nautilus Press, Inc.), 1970-1975.

Scott, Randall W., editor, *Management & Control of Growth,* Vol. I (Washington, D.C.: The Urban Land Institute, 1975a).

Scott, Randall W., editor, *Management & Control of Growth,* Vol. II (Washington, D.C.: The Urban Land Institute, 1975b).

Scott, Randall W., editor, *Management & Control of Growth,* Vol. III (Washington, D.C.: The Urban Land Institute, 1975c).

Seldin, Maury and Swesnik, Richard, *Real Estate Investment Strategy* (New York, N.Y.: Wiley-Interscience, Inc., 1970).

Shabman, Leonard A., "Toward Effective Public Participation in Coastal Zone Management," *Coastal Zone Management Journal,* Vol. I, No. 2, Winter 1974.

Smith, Bernard, "Options for Implementation," *Third Annual National Coastal Zone Management Conference (Asilomar, Calif.: Office of Coastal Zone Management,* NOAA, U.S. Department of Commerce), May 1975.

Sorensen, Jens C., *A Framework for Identification and Control of Resource Degradation & Conflict in the Multiple Use of the Coastal Zone* (Berkeley, Calif.: University of California, 1971).

Sorensen, Jens C., "Coastal Zone Management in California: Three Factors Influencing Future Direction," *Proceedings: Coastal Zone Management and the Western States Future* (Newport Beach, Calif.: Marine Technology Society, December 1973).

Sorensen, Jens C., and Kickert, Thomas, "Social Equity in Coastal Zone Planning," *Coastal Zone Management Journal,* Vol. I, No. 2, Winter 1974.

Sorensen, Jens C. and Demers, Marie, *Coastal Zone Bibliography: Citations to Documents on Planning, Resource Management and Impact Assessment* (Berkeley, Calif.: University of California, 1975).

South Florida Regional Planning Council, "The DRI Process," informational circular (Miami, Fla.: 1973).

Squires, Donald F., "The Coastal Zone-Semantics and Definitions," *Managing Our Coastal Zone* (Albany, N.Y.: New York Sea Grant 1973).

Sternlieb, George, *et al., Housing Development and Municipal Costs* (New Brunswick, N.J.: Center for Urban Policy Research, Rutgers University, 1972).

Stevens, Barbara, "Single-Site Economics in the Construction of Multi-Family Housing," *Land Economics* (Madison, Wis.: University of Wisconsin Press), Vol. LI, No. 1, February 1975.

Sumichrast, Michael and Frankel, Sara A., *Profile of the Builder and His Industry* (Washington, D.C.: National Association of Home Builders, 1970).

Sussna, Stephen, *Land Use Control: More Effective Approaches,* Research Monograph 17 (Washington, D.C.: Urban Land Institute, 1970).

T&M Associates, *Manual of Design Standards, Procedures and Construction Specifications* (Middletown Township, N.J.: Monmouth County, January 1975).

Texas Law Institute of Coastal and Marine Resources, *Comparative Aspects of Coastal Zone Management: Background Information on the Law of Texas and Other States in View of the Coastal Zone Management Act of 1972* (Houston, Tex.: University of Houston, August 1973).

Thurow, Charles, *Performance Controls for Sensitive Lands,* Report Nos. 307 and 308 (Chicago, Ill.: Planning Advisory Service, 1975).

U.S. Department of Housing and Urban Development, "Environmental Review Procedures," *Federal Register,* Vol. 39, No. 198, October 10, 1974.

U.S. House of Representatives, "Legislative History of Coastal Zone Management Act of 1972," *U.S. Code, Congressional and Administrative News, 92nd Congress—Second Session,* Report No. 92-1049 (Washington, D.C.: U.S. Government Printing Office, May 1972).

U.S. National Council on Marine Resources and Engineering Development, *Marine Science Affairs: Selecting Priority Programs* (Washington, D.C.: 1970).

U.S. National Oceanic and Atmospheric Administration, "Coastal Zone Management Program Development Grants," *Federal Register,* Vol. 35, No. 229, November 29, 1972.

U.S. National Oceanic and Atmospheric Administration, "Coastal Zone Management Program Administrative Grants," *Federal Register,* Vol. 40, No. 6, January 9, 1975.

U.S. Senate, "Legislative History of Coastal Zone Management Act of 1972," *U.S. Code, Congressional and Administrative News, 92nd-Congress—Second Session* (St. Paul, Minn.: West Publishing Co., 1973), Vol. 3, p. 4777.

Valentine, David W., *et al., Ecological Surveys for Industrial Sites,* Engineering Bulletin 43 (Los Angeles, Calif.: Dames & Moore, December 1973).

Warren, Robert, Moss, Mitchell L., Bish, Robert L., and Craine, Lyle E., *Designing Coastal Management Agencies: Problems in Allocating Coastal Resources* (Los Angeles, Calif.: University of Southern California, Center for Urban Affairs, September 1972).

Water Resources Administration, *Request for Assistance under Section 305 of the Coastal Zone Management Act of 1972, PL. 92-583* (Baltimore: Maryland Department of Natural Resources, March 1974).

Weicher, John C. and Simonson, John C., "Recent Trends in Housing Costs," *Journal of Economics and Business* (Philadelphia, Pa.: School of Business Administration, Temple University), Vol. 27, No. 2, Winter 1975.

Whitney, Scott, "Siting of Energy Facilities in the Coastal Zone—A Critical Regulatory Hiatus," *William and Mary Law Review* (Williamsburg, Va.: The Marshall-Wythe School of Law, College of William and Mary), Vol. XVI, No. 4, Summer 1975.

Wiesenfeld, Joel, "A Road Map Through New Jersey's Environmental Regulations." A paper presented at the First Annual Drainage Conference at Rutgers University, October 24, 1974.

Wells, Roger, "The Power of Water in Planning," *Landscape Architecture*, January 1974, pp. 21-26.

Yearwood, Richard M., *Land Subdivision Regulation* (New York: Praeger Publishers, 1971).

Yeargan, Percy B., "When Does the Real Estate Seller Make His Profit?" *Real Estate Review*, Vol. 4, No. 3, Fall 1974.

INTERVIEWS:

Angster, Edward, Angster Engineering Inc., Interview, March 20, 1975.

Aversa, Patsy, Realtor, Interview, March 5, 1975.

Badach, Francis, Giodano & Halleran Attorneys at Law, Interview, March 12, 1975.

Bathgate, Lawrence, Bathgate, Wegner, & Sacks Attorneys at Law, Interview, March 17, 1975 and April 18, 1975.

Bellis, Richard, Pollution Control, Division of Water Resources, New Jersey Department of Environmental Protection, Interview, January 13, 1975.

Bernstein, Daniel S., Sacher, Bernstien & Rothberg Attorneys at Law, Interview, May 19, 1975.

Binetsky, Richard N., Chief, Bureau of Regional Planning Division of State & Regional Planning, New Jersey Department of Community Affairs, Interview, May 20, 1975.

Blum, C.B., Dover Township Engineer, T & M Associates Inc., Interview, March 19, 1975.

Borden, Howard, Attorney at Law, Interview, March 20, 1975.

Bottazzi, Patrick, Overland Construction Company, Interview, March 12, 1975.

Broome, John, Administrative Engineer, Dover Sewerage Authority, Interview, March 18, 1975.

Carracino, Joseph, Ernst, Ernst & Lissenden, Interview, April 9, 1975 and March 19, 1975.

Corbet, Marge, Silver Bay Homes Realty, Interview, April 9, 1975 and March 19, 1975.

Curtis, John W., Environmental Assessment Council Inc., Interview, March 8, 1975.

DiSabatino, Gregory, Scarbourgh Corporation, Interview, April 11, 1975.

Dryla, Walter J., Supervisor, CAFRA Permit Section, Division of Marine Services, New Jersey Department of Environmental Protection, Interview, May 20, 1975.

Ernst, John III, Ernst, & Lissenden, Interview, March 6, 1975.

Feehan, Harry, Legal Consul, Office of Coastal Zone Management, NOAA, U.S. Department of Commerce, Interview, June 13, 1975.

Fertakos, James, Gold Crest Construction Company, Interview, March 13, 1975.

Fienberg, Edward, Office of Environmental Analysis, New Jersey Dept. of Environmental Protection, Interview, May 2, 1975.

Filler, Martin, Leisure Technology Corporation, Interview, March 18, 1975.

Frake, Robert, Tax Assessor, Brick Township, Interview, November 29, 1975.

Gargan, Francis, Secretary, Dover Township Shade Tree Commission, Interview, April 19, 1975.

Gold, Dov, Realtor, Baywood Homes, Interview, April 11, 1975.

Goldstein, Fred, Agent for Sleepy Hollow Estates, Interview, March 17, 1975.

Graham, Donald, Director, Division of Marine Services, New Jersey Department of Environmental Protection, Interview, May 20, 1975.

Guerrieri, Rocco, Environmental Specialist, New Jersey Department of Environmental Protection, Interview, April 24, 1975.

Guido, Alfred T., Division of Parks and Forestry, New Jersey Department of Environmental Protection, Interview, February 6, 1975.

Hacunda, Paul, Wilcox, Gravatt & Hacunda, Interview, March 14, 1975.

Hampton, Thomas, Supervisor, Wetlands Section, Division of Marine Services, New Jersey Department of Environmental Protection, Interview, August 26, 1975.

Hankin, Walter, Hankin & Hyres, Interview, April 3, 1975.

Harris, Richard, Lumberman's Mortgage Company, Interview, March 5, 1975.

Havey, James H., Mauro, Havey & Barry Attorneys at Law, Interview, April 8, 1975.

Henry, Capt. B. Russell, Marine Law Enforcement, Division of Marine Services, New Jersey Department of Environmental Protection, Interview, February 6, 1975.

Hirshblond, Manuel, Dover Township Administrator, Interview, April 28, 1975.

Hofman, Richard, Bureau of Floodplains Management, Division of Water Resources, New Jersey Department of Environmental Protection, Interview, March 6, 1975.

Jacobus, Mike, Horne, Tyson & Associates, Interview, March 13, 1975.

Johnson, James, Supervisor, Riparian Section, Division of Marine Services, New Jersey Department of Environmental Protection, Interview, June 10, 1975.

Kelsey, Jack, Realtor, Interview, March 5, 1975.

Kier, William, California Senate Office of Research, Interview, June 13, 1975.

Kinsey, David, New Jersey Department of Environmental Protection, Interview, June 24, 1975.

Kligman, Joel, Suburban Estates, Interview, April 14, 1975.

Kotzas, Byron, Crossroads Realty, Interview, March 19, 1975.

Lane, Richard E., Ocean County Engineer, Interview April 4, 1975.

Lind, Bernard, Bureau of Solid Waste Management, Division of Water Resources, New Jersey Department of Environmental Protection, Interview, January 13, 1975.

McCandless, Thomas C., Dover Township Tax Assessor, Interview, March 19, 1975 and April 23, 1975.

McDonough, William R., Financial Economists, Federal Reserve Bank of Dallas, Texas, Interview, May 26, 1975.

Messano, Alfred L., Alfred L. Messano & Associates, Interview, March 11 and April 8, 1975.

Moore, Bernard, Supervisor, Office of Shore Protection, Division of Marine Services, New Jersey Department of Environmental Protection, Interview, January 10, 1975.

Nelson, Robert A., Ackerman-Ney Associates, Interview, March 18, 1975.

Nouins, Louis, Le Compte Realty, Interview, March 12, 1975.

O'Conner, Dan, Fellows, Read & Weber, Interview, March 12, 1975.

Palmer, Richard, Citta Realty, Interview, March 5, 1975.

Paschon, Robert V., Paschon & Grunin Attorneys at Law, Interview, March 3 and 17, 1975.

Paulson, Glenn L., Assistant Commissioner for Science, New Jersey Department of Environmental Protection, Interview, March 19, 1975.

Penci, Louis M., Donald W. Smith Associates, Interview, March 10 and 18, 1975.

Pograsky, Alan J., Attorney at Law, Interview, April 21, 1975.

Poinsett, David, Historic Sites Section, Division of Parks and Forestry, New Jersey Department of Environmental Protection, Interview, March 6, 1975.

Post, Carl, Architect, Interview, April 8, 1975.

Powers, Robert B., Central Jersey Engineering Inc., Interview, March 13, 1975.

Rahenkamp, John, Rahenkamp, Sachs, Wells & Associates, Interview, July 25, 1975.

Rosentrab, Mark, Institute for Urban Studies, University of Texas, Interview, July 28, 1975.

Russell, Marcus H., Russell and Russ, Interview, March 5 and 11, 1975.

Russo, John, Russo & Courtney Attorneys at Law, Interview, April 23, 1975.

Sebring, Ron, Raymond P. Dinklage Architects, Interview, March 10, 1975.

Shepard, Bruce, Shepard & Hedges, Interview, March 3 and 11, 1975.

Silverman, Arnold, American Planned Communities, Interview, March 7, 1975.

Smith, Donald W., Donald W. Smith and Associates, Interview, April 8, 1975.

Sobel, Martin, Total Building Systems Inc., Interview, March 18, 1975.

Sun, John, Northeast Regional Coordinator, Office of Coastal Zone Management, NOAA, U.S. Department of Commerce, Interview, June 13, 1975.

Tamburro, Florence, Meta Systems Inc., Interview, May 16, 1975.

Tetley, Michele, Information Officer, Office of Coastal Zone Management, NOAA, U.S. Department of Commerce, Interview, June 13, 1975.

Tornopsky, Murry, Building and Land Technology Corporation, Interview, April 9, 1975.

Weinberg, Norman, Director, The Real Estate Institute, New York University, Interview, June 27, 1975.

Wilford, John, Water Supply and Flood Plains, Division of Water Resources, New Jersey Department of Environmental Protection, Interview, March 13, 1975.

Underhill, Richard, Alfred L. Messano & Associates, Interview March 8, 1975.

Yoder, J. Lester, Attorney at Law, Interview, April 9, 1975.

York, Harvey, Novins, Novins, Farley, Grossman & York, Interview, March 20, 1975.

Appendix A
Survey Questionnaire

Interview Identification Number _____

Name _____

Name of Firm _____

The Development

1. Name _____

2. Location (Municipality of
   taxation and zoning power) _____

3. County _____ _____

Land Acquisition

4. Date of purchase—tract(s) _____

5. Identify the buyer and seller _____
   _____

6. Number of Acres in the tract _____

7. $/acre of original purchase _____

8. When you purchased this land for the development, was it zoned
   the same as it is now, did you apply for a variance to change the

requirements or did the requirements change prior to final subdivision approval?

9.   If you applied for a variance what costs did the project incure? __

_____

Same _____

Variance _____

Change _____

Subdivision or Site Plan

10.   Considerable modification has occurred in the subdivision and
      site plan process during the last thirty years. Below is a list of
      descriptive characteristics pertaining to each subsequent sub-
      division or site plan of the development, we would like you to fill
      in the respective data pertaining to each plat you designed.

Characteristic	Subdivision or Site Plan
Acreage	
Number of lots	
Lot size	
Acreage in street	
Acreage in lots	
Unimproved filed Lot selling price	

11.   Processing of subdivision plans often involves much governmen-
      tal delay. For each subdivision or site plan, have you experienced
      many delays in approval of plat designs and/or any other required
      approvals? (Yes or No)

      _____

12. Please specify what major areas of delay occurred and the number of months required for their processing.

_____

_____

_____

_____

_____

13. How long did it take you to obtain all necessary approvals and permits so you could proceed with site preparation?
    (dates) _____
    (months) _____

14. Are all subdivision costs represented in the price of the filed un-improved lots or have you absorbed some of the costs?

_____

15. If yes, could you approximate the percentage of subdivision costs reflected in lot selling price._____(%)

16. Land development costs include fees charged by political sub-divisions to cover the administrative costs of subdivision-site plan approval and permit applications. Below is a list of items often charged to the developer by the township, county, and state. Please fill in the appropriate charge as applicable to each subdivision or site plan and note any additional engineering, architectural, inspection, legal, and/or consulting costs incurred by the project to meet the regulation.

Approval Processing of Subdivision or Site Plan

ITEM	TIME	UNITS	COSTS	FEES
Dover Township:				
Sketch plat				
preliminary plat				
final plat				
inspection				
site plan review				
site plan approval				
inspection				
reproduction costs				
zoning variances				
use permit				
sewer connection				
preliminary sewer plan				
tentative sewer plan				
final sewer plan				
sewer inspection				
cash sewer bond				
performance sewer bond				
septic system permit				
percolation tests				
water system review				
water connection				
well permit				
fire commission review				
soil-land disturbance permit				
tree removal permit				
shade tree bond				
wetlands permit				
floodplain permit				
building demolition permit				
cash improvement bond				
performance improvement bond				

Ocean County:

subdivision review				
site plan review				
drainage assessment				
sewer system permit				
road trench opening permit				

State of New Jersey:

riparian rights permit				
wetlands permit				
CAFRA permit				
stream encroachment permit				
individual well permit				
private groundwater diversion permit				
private surface water diversion permit				
public water diversion permit				
public water system permit				
public sewer system permit				
individual sewer system permit				
septic sewer system permit				
hotel and multiple dwelling permit				
retirement community registration				
condominium review				
road access permit				
road attachment permit				
road drainage permit				
use of right-of-way permit				
utility opening permit				

Developer Carrying Costs

17. What is the property tax per year on the tract? _____

18. What is your equity investment and expected rate of return on that investment?

     equity _____

     rate of return _____

19. What annual interest charges do you pay on the mortgage and
     what is the annual interest rate?

          mortgage _____
          rate of interest _____
          interest charge _____

20. For what period is the mortgage outstanding? _____

21. What additional carrying costs are affecting the project?

SUBDIVISION PROCESSING TIME

Item

Month/Year

Appendix B

Data Matrices

Four data matrices are presented in this appendix:

1. Regulatory costs per unit borne by the developer and processing time in months, subdivision process (single family developments)

2. Regulatory costs per unit borne by the developer and processing time in months, site plan process (multi-family developments)

3. Total costs per unit incurred by the developer, subdivision process (single family developments)

4. Total costs per unit incurred by the developer, site plan process (multi-family developments)

The first matrix begins on the following page.

REGULATORY COSTS PER UNIT
BORNE BY THE DEVELOPER AND PROCESSING
TIME IN MONTHS, SUBDIVISION PROCESS
(SINGLE FAMILY DEVELOPMENTS)

		1		2		3	
Coastal Zone	*Project Number:*						
Land Use	*Number of Units:*	83		47		144	
Regulations	*Number of Acres:*	32.7		34.2		78.1	
	Average Lot Size:	17,500'		18,000'		18,000'	
		Cost	Time	Cost	Time	Cost	Time
TOWNSHIP:							
Utilities:							
Telephone Company		---	1	---	1	---	1
Electric Company		---	1	---	1	---	1
Water Company		---	1	---	1	---	1
Fire Commission Review		9.10	1	5.58	1	---	1
Preliminary Sewer Review		10.06	17	8.03	4	9.46	1
Tentative Sewer Review		18.71	27	10.76	1	11.46	2
Final Sewer Review		31.96	25	18.91	1	15.79	1
Sewer Inspection Fee		94.06	-	47.19	-	62.29	1
Sewer Connection Fee		250.00	-	250.00	-	138.89	-
Cash Sewer Bond		130.23	24	65.34	-	95.87	2
Performance Sewer Bond		19.75	24	9.91	-	17.94	2
Plans Review:							
Sketch Plat		73.87	5	40.54	-	54.51	4
Tentative (Preliminary) Plat		133.41	13	100.14	7	110.80	4
Final Plat		146.23	31	118.23	13	114.27	5
Engineering Fee to Township		175.00	-	212.77	-	183.33	-
Zoning Variance or Use Permit		---	-	---	-	---	-
Cash Improvement Bond		329.74	8	902.40	-	403.04	-
Performance Bond		41.18	8	82.02	-	54.41	-
Environmental:							
Land or Soil Disturbance Permit		9.19	1	5.58	1	---	1
Tree Removal Permit		22.67	11	25.27	13	20.49	4
Wetlands Permit		14.04	1	13.46	14	10.07	1
Flood Fringe Permit		---	-	---	-	8.11	1
Shade Tree Bond		4.39	2	5.66		3.62	2
COUNTY:							
Plans Review:							
Sketch, Preliminary, and Final		4.95	1	3.00	1	3.13	1
Utilities:							
Drainage Assessment		labor	8	...	1	---	1
Sewer System Permit		1.58	1	2.13	1	0.69	1
STATE:							
Plans Review:							
CAFRA Permit (Coastal Area Facility Review Act)		29.67	9	87.16	11	29.17	19
Total Unit Cost of Coastal Zone Land Use Regulations		540.77		2008.58		1347.42	
Total Project Duration in Months			50		37		25

Dover Township, Ocean County, New Jersey
data collected: February-May 1975
developments: CAFRA applicants, September 1973-April 1975

1. All figures adjusted by ratios in Figure 4.8
2. Italics are estimated by cost sources such as
   review agency, consultants, and/or developer.

REGULATORY COSTS PER UNIT
BORNE BY THE DEVELOPER AND PROCESSING
TIME IN MONTHS, SUBDIVISION PROCESS
(SINGLE FAMILY DEVELOPMENTS) (Cont'd.)

4 / 28 / 7.9 / 7,500'		5 / 35 / 11.3 / 12,000'		6 / 96 / 43.5 / 15,000'		7 / 36 / 18.0 / 14,000'		8 / 109 / 39.0 / 9,000'		9 / 313 / 400.0 / 45,000'		10 / 72 / 44.5 / 20,000'		11 / 89 / 10.5 / 11,000'		Average / 89 / 65.4 / 17,000'	
Cost	Time	Cost	Time	Cost	Time	Cost	Time	Cost	Time	Cost	Time	Cost	Time	Cost	Time	Cost	Time
---	1	---	1	---	1	---	1	---	1	---	1	---	1	---	1	---	1
---	1	---	1	---	1	---	1	---	1	---	1	---	1	---	1	---	1
---	1	---	1	---	1	---	1	---	1	---	1	---	1	---	1	---	1
5.57	-	6.59	1	6.63	1	10.50	1	6.50	1	12.46	1	5.53	1	5.67	1	7.42	1
8.21	1	8.80	1	8.82	1	11.06	1	8.62	1	12.19	1	8.26	1	8.40	1	9.26	1
15.05	1	10.30	1	10.36	-	7.74	-	7.74	1	13.93	2	9.35	-	9.61	1	11.36	1
24.93	1	18.26	1	18.34	-	16.04	-	14.13	-	24.73	5	16.38	-	16.81	1	19.66	1
73.97	1	44.37	1	47.45	-	18.75	-	30.41	1	46.93	-	44.24	-	42.66	1	50.21	1
250.00	-	258.57	-	250.00	-	250.00	-	250.00	-	---	-	250.00	-	250.00	-	239.74	1
102.43	-	68.14	2	65.70	-	28.83	-	37.43	-	36.10	2	68.06	-	65.64	-	69.43	2
15.54	-	9.43	2	9.96	-	3.90	-	6.47	-	---	2	9.19	-	8.85	-	11.09	2
44.79	2	53.00	3	53.27	-	84.41	-	47.94	-	100.24	-	44.46	1	45.55	3	58.42	3
101.00	7	82.60	3	96.08	13	177.41	3	109.55	2	232.07	5	144.71	7	109.37	10	127.01	7
105.79	2	94.11	5	98.43	-	166.96	3	98.30	3	237.80	5	117.21	-	95.82	5	126.65	5
225.00	-	200.00	-	175.00	-	200.00	-	150.00	-	175.00	-	175.00	-	200.00	-	188.28	-
---	-	36.67	1	---	-	---	-	46.10	5	---	-	---	-	---	-	---	-
494.64	-	378.00	3	664.58	-	330.56	-	653.94	1	613.74	-	667.36	-	230.77	2	515.34	1
50.97	-	32.14	3	59.09	-	43.88	-	55.60	1	82.85	-	60.20	-	35.00	2	54.30	1
5.57	-	6.59	1	6.63	1	10.50	1	6.50	1	12.46	1	5.53	1	5.67	1	7.42	1
13.79	-	16.43	2	19.10	25	15.30	1	15.37	6	22.93	5	22.22	19	24.06	14	19.78	8
14.21	-	10.51	4	19.61	24	---	-	15.83	6	23.89	5	22.65	-	14.24	13	15.85	6
---	-	---	-	---	-	---	-	---	-	---	1	---	1	---	-	8.11	1
1.53	1	70.09	2	3.69	-	32.98	1	3.28	1	3.47	1	3.68	-	3.69	-	12.37	1
3.00	1	3.55	1	3.57	1	5.65	1	3.50	-	6.71	1	2.98	1	3.05	1	3.92	1
---	1	100.00	1	---	1	44.44	1	labor	1	---	1	37.15	1	---	1	60.53	1
3.57	1	2.86	1	1.04	1	2.78	1	0.92	1	0.32	1	1.39	1	2.56	1	1.80	1
71.43	14	41.43	14	44.79	15	91.25	13	44.27	11	30.35	14	28.93	15	51.28	15	49.98	12
1624.79	28	1509.95	26	1655.59	35	1542.52	24	1605.98	31	1675.50	26	1739.03	39	1224.72	22	1588.62	30

THE COST OF ENVIRONMENTAL PROTECTION

REGULATORY COSTS PER UNIT
BORNE BY THE DEVELOPER AND PROCESSING
TIME IN MONTHS, SITE PLAN PROCESS
(MULTI-FAMILY DEVELOPMENTS)

Coastal Zone Land Use Regulations		*l3*		*l4*		*l5*	
Project Number:		*l3*		*l4*		*l5*	
Number of Units:		*348*		*38*		*110*	
Number of Acres:		*43.8*		*4.1*		*27.0*	
		Cost	Time	Cost	Time	Cost	Time
TOWNSHIP:							
Utilities:							
Telephone Company		---	1	---	1	---	1
Electric Company		---	1	---	1	---	1
Water Company		---	1	---	1	---	1
Fire Commission Review		0.97	2	3.97	1	7.64	1
Preliminary Sewer Review		5.56	1	7.29	1	9.45	-
Tentative Sewer Review		4.30	1	7.84	-	9.89	-
Final Sewer Review		6.86	2	13.45	-	18.07	-
Sewer Inspection Fee		23.50	-	36.69	-	41.36	-
Sewer Connection Fee		250.00	-	250.00	-	250.00	-
Cash Sewer Bond		128.02	-	50.80	-	57.27	-
Performance Sewer Bond		17.19	-	7.89	-	8.69	-
Plans Review:							
Sketch Site Plan		7.81	-	31.92	12	61.43	-
Site Plan Review		30.59	9	174.92	10	213.19	
Zoning Variance		6.48	6	72.11	3	30.00	7
Improvement Bond		17.19	-	37.91	-	27.00	-
Environmental:							
Land or Soil Disturbance Permit		4.30	7	8.02	8	15.25	1
Tree Removal Permit		3.24	3	8.33	1	15.84	1
COUNTY:							
Plans Review:							
Sketch and Site Plan Review		0.52	1	2.14	1	4.11	2
Utilities:							
Drainage Assessment		---	1	---	-	labor	2
Sewer System Permit		0.29	1	2.63	-	0.91	-
STATE:							
Plans Review:							
CAFRA Permit (Coastal Area Facility Review Act)		12.93	*10*	89.85	12	43.41	12
Total Unit Cost of Coastal Zone Land Use Regulation		519.75		805.76		877.14	
Total Project Duration in Months			31		31		21

Dover Township, Ocean County, New Jersey
data collected: February-May 1975
developments: CAFRA applicants, September 1973-April 1975

1. All figures adjusted by ratios in Figure 4.8
2. Italics are estimated by cost sources such as review agency, consultants, and/or developer

REGULATORY COSTS PER UNIT
BORNE BY THE DEVELOPER AND PROCESSING
TIME IN MONTHS, SITE PLAN PROCESS
(MULTI-FAMILY DEVELOPMENTS) (Cont'd.)

	16 — 72 — 9.0		17 — 276 — 46.3		18 — 160 — 25.7		19 — 184 — 23		20 — 62 — 10.4		21 — 560 — 84.9		Average — 201 — 30.5		Commercial Development — 129 — 5.3	
	Cost	Time	Cost	Time	Cost	Time	Cost	Time	Cost	Time	Cost	Time	Cost	Time	Cost	Time
	---	1	---	1	---	1	---	1	---	1	---	1	---	1	---	1
	---	1	---	1	---	1	---	1	---	1	---	1	---	1	---	1
	---	1	---	1	---	1	---	1	---	1	---	1	---	1	---	1
	4.01	1	1.21	2	3.21	5	1.64	1	3.44	1	1.13	1	3.02	1	1.44	1
	7.31	1	5.70	1	6.85	1	5.95	1	6.99	2	5.65	2	6.75	1	6.65	2
	7.54	3	5.30	-	8.05	-	2.50	-	4.20	2	5.88	-	6.17	2	.86	-
	13.01	3	8.47	-	13.43	-	4.44	-	7.76	2	9.30	-	10.53	2	1.90	-
	34.40	-	30.82	-	42.97	-	11.30	-	15.96	2	34.82	-	30.20	2	1.26	-
	250.00	-	250.00	-	250.00	-	250.00	-	250.00	-	250.00	-	250.00	2	323.64	-
	47.63	1	42.68	-	59.08	-	17.39	-	24.55	-	53.57	-	53.44	1	1.94	-
	7.22	1	6.47	-	8.96	-	2.35	-	3.31	-	7.23	-	7.70	1	.26	-
	32.22	4	14.56	4	25.82	-	13.19	-	27.67	8	9.11	-	24.86	4	11.60	-
	154.11	5	36.93	13	118.05	10	63.93	8	131.39	8	39.86	9	107.00	8	42.32	2
	72.68	8	9.11	11	27.11	13	21.18	4	26.67	7	15.76	9	31.23	7	35.27	6
	31.25	1	22.17	-	36.56	-	24.46	-	25.89	-	29.46	-	27.99	1	16.98	-
	8.25	5	5.70	5	7.89	10	5.08	1	8.54	8	5.15		7.58	8	3.08	12
	6.13	5	4.17	6	4.23	2	5.21	1	6.39	8	5.23		6.53	6		-
	2.16	1	0.65	4	1.73	1	0.88	1	1.85	1	0.61	1	1.63	1	0.82	2
	labor	1	---	1	---	1	---	2	labor		---	1	---	1	---	2
	1.39	1	0.36	-	0.63	1	0.54	-	1.61		0.18	1	0.95	1	0.78	
	31.94	4	11.39	10	31.25	15	24.42	10	47.54	9	7.05	7	33.30	10	23.26	8
	711.25	25	455.63	24	667.85	25	454.46	19	593.76	19	479.99	18	676.59	24	472.06	25

TOTAL COSTS PER UNIT
INCURRED BY THE DEVELOPER, SUBDIVISION
PROCESS (SINGLE FAMILY DEVELOPMENTS)

Costs and Rates for Expenses Incurred during the Subdivision Process	Project Number: / Project Duration (months): / method of Land acquisition:	1 / 50 / held prior to subdivision		2 / 37 / downpayment and mortgage		3 / 25 / downpayment and mortgages*		4 / 28 / downpayment and mortgages		5 / 26 / downpayment and mortgages	
		Cost	Rate	Cost	Rate	Cost	Rate	Cost	Rate	Cost	Rate
Cost of Raw Land:											
Purchase Price at Commencement of Process		958.99		2,245.48		1,626.04		3,113.74		3,522.40	
Downpayment		958.99	100%	651.19	29%	325.21	20%	970.88	31%	479.55	14%
Mortgages: one:		-		1,594.29	71%	1,300.83	80%	2,142.86	69%	3,042.85	86%
(or note) two:		-		-		1,250.00		-		-	
three:		-				2,805.56					
four:		-				1,013.88					
Interest Rate of Mortgages: One:		-					8%				
(or note) two:		-							7.5%		9%
three:		-							8%		
four:		-							10%		
Mortgage Terms: :one:		-		60 months		60 months		12 months		16 months	
(months) (or note) two:		-		-		60 months		-		-	
three:		-		-		60 months		-		-	
four:		-		-		18 months		-		-	
Interest Costs:											
Total charges incurred during Subdivision Process		-		273.80		430.28		88.03		188.60	
Taxes:											
Tax payment during the Subdivision Process		145.96		75.41		42.07		66.62		167.23	
Cost of Coastal Zone Land Use Regulations:											
Total costs of all consultants and paperwork		1,540.77		2,008.58		1,347.42		1,624.79		1,509.95	
Carrying Costs:											
Rate Quoted by Developer			15%				28%		20%		15%
Costs at 15 percent[1]		919.65		631.13		360.87		1,136.74		557.63	
Costs at 20 percent		1,226.20		841.51		481.16		1,515.65		743.51	
Approved Unit Costs:[3]											
Total of all Expenses Incurred by Developer		3,631.74		5,234.40		3,806.68		6,029.92		5,945.81	
Approved, Yet Unimproved Unit Selling Price:[2]											
Unit Cost of "Packaged" Land		5,500.00		6,500.00		6,500.00		5,800.00		6,500.00	

Dover Township, Ocean County, New Jersey
data collected: February - May, 1975
developments: CAFRA applicants September, 1973 - April, 1975

[1] 15 percent carrying costs used in all calculations and totals

[2] Actual sales or realistic prices sought by developer

[3] Approved Unit Costs include the cost of land, taxes, interest, regulations, and carrying investment at 15 percent

[4] This project was purchased during the course of its subdivision process and financed by a series of mortgages. Italics are estimated by developer

TOTAL COSTS PER UNIT
INCURRED BY THE DEVELOPER, SUBDIVISION
PROCESS (SINGLE FAMILY DEVELOPMENTS) (Cont'd.)

6 35 downpayment and mortgage		7 24 held prior to subdivision		8 31¹ downpayment and mortgage		9 26 downpayment and mortgage		10 30 downpayment and mortgage and note		11 22 downpayment and mortgage		Average 30 downpayment and mortgage	
Cost	Rate	Cost	Rate	Cost	Rate	Cost	Rate	Cost	Rate	Cost	Rate	Cost	Rate
1,378.69		1,444.44		3,173.23		2,571.25		2,915.96		2,564.10		2,319.48	
399.82	29%	1,444.44	100%	475.98	15%	2,507.35	97%	463.00	16%	717.95	28%	672.65	29%
978.87	71%	0		2,697.25	85%	63.90	3%	1,133.53	39%	1,846.15	72%	1,646.83	71%
-		-		-		-		1,319.44	45%	-		-	
-		-		-		-		-		-		-	
-	6.75%	-		-	7.5%	-	5%	-	8%	-	7.5%	-	8%
-		-		-		-		-	9%	-		-	
-		-		-		-		-		-		-	
60 months		-		48months		36 months		36 months 90 day note		36 months		60 months	
-		-		-		-		-		-		-	
-		-		-		-		-		-		-	
177.33		-		320.48		4.62		140.30		184.74		200.91	
97.60		134.16		79.85		29.64		121.40		63.15		93.01	
1,655.59		1,542.52		1,605.98		1,675.50		1,739.03		1,224.72		1,588.62	
	15%		20%		12%		15%		15%		20%		17.5%
699.72		635.01		579.23		951.66		574.83		480.17			15%
932.96		846.68		772.31		1,268.88		766.44		640.23			20%
4,008.93		3,756.13		5,758.77		5,232.67		5,491.52		4,516.88		4,855.77	
5,250.00		6,500.00		6,500.00		6,800.00		5,500.00		4,500.00		5,868.18	

TOTAL COSTS PER UNIT
INCURRED BY THE DEVELOPER, SITE PLAN
PROCESS (MULTI-FAMILY DEVELOPMENTS)

Costs and Rates for *Expenses Incurred during* *the Site Plan Process*	*Project Number:* *Project (months):* *method of* *land acquisition:*		*13* *31* *downpayment* *and mortgage*		*14* *31* *downpayment* *and note*		*15* *21* *downpayment* *and mortgage*		*16*[1] *25* *purchase* *option*	
		Cost	Rate	Cost	Rate	Cost	Rate	Cost	Rate
Cost of Raw Land:										
Purchase Price at Commencement of Process		440.52		2,236.84		859.09		1,125.00	
Downpayment:		223.44	51%	1,052.63	47%	515.45	60%	902.77	29%
Mortgage:		217.08	49%			343.64	40%	-	
Note:		-		1,184.21	53%	-		2,194.44	71%
Options for Purchase:		-		-		-		22.55	
Interest Rate of Mortgage or Note			7.5%		8%		0		11.75%
Term of Mortgage or Note		60 months		90 day renew		120 months		15 months	
Interest Costs:									
Total charges incurred during Site Plan Process		69.96		244.78		-		138.48	
Taxes									
Tax payment during the Site Plan Process		41.37		156.95		58.23		39.47	
Cost of Coastal Zone Land Use Regulations									
Total costs of all consultants and paperwork		519.75		805.76		877.14		711.25	
Carrying Costs:									
Rate Quoted by Developer			15%		15%		15%		20%
Costs at 15 percent [2]		327.98		488.84		401.27		311.30	
Costs at 20 percent		437.31		651.79		535.03		415.07	
Approved Unit Costs:[4]									
Total of all Expenses incurred by Developer		1,399.58		3,933.17		2,195.73		2,325.50	
Approved, Yet Unimproved Unit Selling Price:[3]									
Unit Cost of "Packaged"Land		3,500.00		4,000.00		3,800.00		3,097.22	

Dover Township, Ocean County, New Jersey
    data collected: February - May, 1975
    developments: CAFRA applicants September, 1973 - April, 1975

[1] This project was purchased during the course of its site plan process and financed by
    a down payment and mortgage or note arrangement.

[2] 15 percent carrying costs used in all calculations and totals

[3] Actual sales or realistic prices sought by developer.

[4] Approved Unit Costs include the cost of land, taxes, interest, regulations and
    carrying investment at 15 percent.

TOTAL COSTS PER UNIT
INCURRED BY THE DEVELOPER, SITE PLAN
PROCESS (MULTI-FAMILY DEVELOPMENTS) (Cont'd.)

	17 / 24 downpayment and mortgage		18 / 25 downpayment and mortgage		19 / 19 purchase option		20 / 19 downpayment and mortgage		21 / 18 downpayment and mortgage		Average 24		Commercial Development 25 downpayment and mortgage	
	Cost	Rate	Cost	Rate	Cost	Rate	Cost	Rate	Cost	Rate	Cost	Rate	Cost	Rate
	1,014.49		1,124.38		3,472.83		670.97		535.36		1,275.50		1,021.71	
	724.64	71%	1,074.38	96%	570.66	16%	194.58	29%	155.25	29%	369.90	29%	204.35	
	289.85	29%	50.00	4%	2,902.17	84%	476.39	71%	380.11	71%	905.60	71%	817.36	
	-		-		-		-		-		-		-	
	-		-		114.13		-		-		-		-	
		11.5%		8%		7%		8%		8.5%		8%		9.75%
	24 months		60 months		18 months		60 months		120 months		60 months		36 months	
	36.07		6.90		-		49.55		35.27		83.00		68.87	
	14.30		15.74		86.75		39.52		15.60		51.99		74.96	
	455.63		667.85		454.46		593.76		479.99		676.59		472.06	
		15%		15%		-		-		15%		15%		15%
	298.21		399.12		140.96		125.01		99.69		287.52		304.13	
	390.95		532.16		187.95		166.68		132.92		383.36		405.51	
	1,813.70		2,213.99		4,155.00		1,478.81		1,165.91		2,297.95		1,941.73	
	4,000.00		4,000.00		4,500.00		3,500.00		3,500.00		3,766.67		3,500.00	

Appendix C

Federal Coastal Zone Management Act

Be it enacted by the Senate and House of Representatives of the United States of America in Congress assembled, That the Act entitled "An Act to provide for a comprehensive, long-range, and coordinated national program in marine science, to establish a National Council on Marine Resources and Engineering Development, and a Commission on Marine Science, Engineering and Resources, and for other purposes", approved June 17, 1966 (80 Stat. 203), as amended (33 U.S.C. 1101-1124), is further amended by adding at the end thereof the following new title:

TITLE III—MANAGEMENT OF THE COASTAL ZONE

SHORT TITLE

SEC. 301. This title may be cited as the "Coastal Zone Management Act of 1972".

CONGRESSIONAL FINDINGS

SEC. 302. The Congress finds that—

(a) There is a national interest in the effective management, beneficial use, protection, and development of the coastal zone; .

(b) The coastal zone is rich in a variety of natural, commercial, recreational, industrial, and esthetic resources of immediate and potential value to the present and future well-being of the Nation;

(c) The increasing and competing demands upon the lands and waters of our coastal zone occasioned by population growth and economic development, including requirements for industry, commerce, residential development, recreation, extraction of mineral resources and fossil fuels, transportation and navigation, waste disposal, and harvesting of fish, shellfish, and other living marine resources, have resulted in the loss of living marine resources, wildlife, nutrient-rich areas, permanent and adverse changes to ecological systems, decreasing open space for public use, and shoreline erosion;

(d) The coastal zone, and the fish, shellfish, other living marine resources, and wildlife therein, are ecologically fragile and consequently extremely vulnerable to destruction by man's alterations;

(e) Important ecological, cultural, historic, and esthetic values in the coastal zone which are essential to the well-being of all citizens are being irretrievably damaged or lost;

(f) Special natural and scenic characteristics are being damaged by ill-planned development that threatens these values;

(g) In light of competing demands and the urgent need to protect and to give high priority to natural systems in the coastal zone, present state and local institutional arrangements for planning and regulating land and water uses in such areas are inadequate; and

(h) The key to more effective protection and use of the land and water resources of the coastal zone is to encourage the states to exercise their full authority over the lands and waters in the coastal zone by assisting the states, in cooperation with Federal and local governments and other vitally affected interests, in developing land and water use programs for the coastal zone, including unified policies, criteria, standards, methods, and processes for dealing with land and water use decisions of more than local significance.

DECLARATION OF POLICY

SEC. 303. The Congress finds and declares that it is the national policy (a) to preserve, protect, develop, and where possible, to restore or enhance, the resources of the Nation's coastal zone for this and succeeding generations, (b) to encourage and assist the states to exercise effectively their responsibilities in the coastal zone through the development and implementation of management programs to achieve wise use of the land and water resources of the coastal zone giving full consideration to ecological, cultural, historic, and esthetic values as well as to needs for economic development, (c) for all Federal agencies engaged in programs affecting the coastal zone to cooperate and participate with state and local governments and regional agencies in effectuating the purposes of this title, and (d) to encourage the participation of the public, of Federal, state, and local governments and of regional agencies in the development of coastal zone management programs. With respect to implementation of such management programs, it is the national policy to encourage cooperation among the various state and regional agencies including establishment of interstate and regional agreements, cooperative procedures, and joint action particularly regarding environmental problems.

DEFINITIONS

SEC. 304. For the purposes of this title—

(a) "Coastal zone" means the coastal waters (including the lands therein and thereunder) and the adjacent shorelands (including the waters therein and thereunder), strongly influenced by each other and in proximity to the shorelines of the several coastal states, and includes transitional and intertidal areas, salt marshes, wetlands, and beaches. The zone extends, in Great Lakes waters, to the international boundary between the United States and Canada and, in other areas, seaward to the outer limit of the United States territorial sea. The zone extends inland from the shorelines only to the extent necessary to control shorelands, the uses of which have a direct and significant impact on the coastal waters. Excluded from the coastal zone are lands the use of which is by law subject solely to the discretion of or which is held in trust by the Federal Government, its officers or agents.

(b) "Coastal waters" means (1) in the Great Lakes area, the waters within the territorial jurisdiction of the United States consisting of the Great Lakes, their connecting waters, harbors, roadsteads, and estuary-type areas such as bays, shallows, and marshes and (2) in other areas, those waters, adjacent to the shorelines, which contain a measurable quantity or percentage of sea water, including, but not limited to, sounds, bays, lagoons, bayous, ponds, and estuaries.

(c) "Coastal state" means a state of the United States in, or bordering on, the Atlantic, Pacific, or Arctic Ocean, the Gulf of Mexico, Long Island Sound, or one or more of the Great Lakes. For the purposes of this title, the term also includes Puerto Rico, the Virgin Islands, Guam, and American Samoa.

(d) "Estuary" means that part of a river or stream or other body of water having unimpaired connection with the open sea, where the sea water is measurably diluted with fresh water derived from land drainage. The term includes estuary-type areas of the Great Lakes.

(e) "Estuarine sanctuary" means a research area which may include any part or all of an estuary, adjoining transitional areas, and adjacent uplands, constituting to the extent feasible a natural unit, set aside to provide scientists and students the opportunity to examine over a period of time the ecological relationships within the area.

(f) "Secretary" means the Secretary of Commerce.

(g) "Management program" includes, but is not limited to, a comprehensive statement in words, maps, illustrations, or other media of communication, prepared and adopted by the state in accordance with the provisions of this title, setting forth objectives, policies, and standards to guide public and private uses of lands and waters in the coastal zone.

(h) "Water use" means activities which are conducted in or on the water; but does not mean or include the establishment of any water quality standard or criteria or the regulation of the discharge or runoff of water pollutants except the standards, criteria, or regulations which are incorporated in any program as required by the provisions of section 307 (f).

(i) "Land use" means activities which are conducted in or on the shorelands within the coastal zone, subject to the requirements outlined in section 307(g).

MANAGEMENT PROGRAM DEVELOPMENT GRANTS

SEC. 305. (1) The Secretary is authorized to make annual grants to any coastal state for the purpose of assisting in the development of a management program for the land and water resources of its coastal zone.

(b) Such management program shall include:

(1) an identification of the boundaries of the coastal zone subject to the management program;

(2) a definition of what shall constitute permissible land and water uses within the coastal zone which have a direct and significant impact on the coastal waters;

(3) an inventory and designation of areas of particular concern within the coastal zone;

(4) an identification of the means by which the state proposes to exert control over the land and water uses referred to in paragraph (2) of this subsection, including a listing of relevant constitutional provisions, legislative enactments, regulations, and judicial decisions;

(5) broad guidelines on priority of uses in particular areas, including specifically those uses of lowest priority;

(6) a description of the organizational structure proposed to implement the management program, including the responsibilities and interrelationships of local, areawide, state, regional, and interstate agencies in the management process.

(c) The grants shall not exceed 66⅔ per centum of the costs of the program in any one year and no state shall be eligible to receive more than three annual grants pursuant to this section. Federal funds received from other sources shall not be used to match such grants. In order to qualify for grants under this section, the state must reasonably demonstrate to the satisfaction of the Secretary that such grants will be used to develop a management program consistent with the requirements set forth in section 306 of this title. After making the initial grant to a coastal state, no subsequent grant shall be made under this section unless the Secretary finds that the state is satisfactorily developing such management program.

(d) Upon completion of the development of the state's management program, the state shall submit such program to the Secretary for review and approval pursuant to the provisions of section 306 of this title, or such other action as he deems necessary. On final approval of such program by the Secretary, the state's eligibility for further grants under this section shall terminate, and the state shall be eligible for grants under section 306 of this title.

(e) Grants under this section shall be allocated to the states based on rules and regulations promulgated by the Secretary: *Provided, however,* That no management program development grant under this section shall be made in excess of 10 per centum nor less than 1 per centum of the total amount appropriated to carry out the purposes of this section.

(f) Grants or portions thereof not obligated by a state during the fiscal year for which they were first authorized to be obligated by the state, or during the fiscal year immediately following, shall revert to the Secretary, and shall be added by him to the funds available for grants under this section.

(g) With the approval of the Secretary, the state may allocate to a local government, to an areawide agency designated under section 204 of the Demonstration Cities and Metropolitan Development Act of 1966, to a regional agency, or to an interstate agency, a portion of the grant under this section, for the purpose of carrying out the provisions of this section.

(h) The authority to make grants under this section shall expire on June 30, 1977.

ADMINISTRATIVE GRANTS

SEC. 306. (1) The Secretary is authorized to make annual grants to any coastal state for not more than 66⅔ per centum of the costs of administering the state's management program, if he approves such program in accordance with subsection (c) hereof. Federal funds received from other sources shall not be used to pay the state's share of costs.

(b) Such grants shall be allocated to the states with approved programs based on rules and regulations promulgated by the Secretary which shall take into account the extent and nature of the shoreline and area covered by the plan, population of the area, and other relevant factors: *Provided, however,* That no annual administrative grant under this section shall be made in excess of 10 per centum nor less than 1 per centum of the total amount appropriated to carry out the purposes of this section.

(c) Prior to granting approval of a management program submitted by a coastal state, the Secretary shall find that:

(1) The state has developed and adopted a management program for its coastal zone in accordance with rules and regulations promulgated by the Secretary, after notice, and with the opportunity of full participation by relevant Federal agencies, state agencies, local governments, regional organizations, port authorities, and other interested parties, public and private, which is adequate to carry out the purposes of this title and is consistent with the policy declared in section 303 of this title.

(2) The state has:

(A) coordinated its program with local, areawide, and interstate plans applicable to areas within the coastal zone existing on January 1 of the year in which the state's management program is submitted to the Secretary, which plans have been developed by a local government, an areawide agency designated pursuant to regulations established under section 204 of the Demonstration Cities and Metropolitan Development Act of 1966, a regional agency, or an interstate agency; and

(B) established an effective mechanism for continuing consultation and coordination between the management agency designated pursuant to paragraph (5) of this subsection and with local governments, interstate agencies, regional agencies, and areawide agencies within the coastal zone to assure the full participation of such local governments and agencies in carrying out the purposes of this title.

(3) The state has held public hearings in the development of the management program.

(4) The management program and any changes thereto have been reviewed and approved by the Governor.

(5) The Governor of the state has designated a single agency to receive and administer the grants for implementing the management program required under paragraph (1) of this subsection.

(6) The state is organized to implement the management program required under paragraph (1) of this subsection.

(7) The state has the authorities necessary to implement the program, including the authority required under subsection (d) of this section.

(8) The management program provides for adequate consideration of the national interest involved in the siting of facilities necessary to meet requirements which are other than local in nature.

(9) The management program makes provision for procedures whereby specific areas may be designated for the purpose of preserving or restoring them for their conservation, recreational, ecological, or esthetic values.

(d) Prior to granting approval of the management program, the Secretary shall find that the state, acting through its chosen agency or agencies, including local governments, areawide agencies designated under section 204 of the Demonstration Cities and Metropolitan Development Act of 1966, regional agencies, or interstate agencies, has authority for the management of the coastal zone in accordance with the management program. Such authority shall include power—

(1) to administer land and water use regulations, control development in order to ensure compliance with the management program, and to resolve conflicts among competing uses; and

(2) to acquire fee simple and less than fee simple interests in lands, waters, and other property through condemnation or other means when necessary to achieve conformance with the management program.

(e) Prior to granting approval, the Secretary shall also find that the program provides:

(1) for any one or a combination of the following general techniques for control of land and water uses within the coastal zone;

(A) State establishment of criteria and standards for local implementation, subject to administrative review and enforcement of compliance;

(B) Direct state land and water use planning and regulation; or

(C) State administrative review for consistency with the management program of all development plans, projects, or land and water use regulations, including exceptions and variances thereto, proposed by any state or local authority or private developer, with power to approve or disapprove after public notice and an opportunity for hearings.

(2) for a method of assuring that local land and water use regulations within the coastal zone do not unreasonably restrict or exclude land and water uses of regional benefit.

(f) With the approval of the Secretary, a state may allocate to a local government, an areawide agency designated under section 204 of the Demonstration Cities and Metropolitan Development Act of 1966, a regional agency, or an interstate agency, a portion of the grant under this section for the purpose of carrying out the provisions of this section: *Provided,* That such allocation shall not relieve the state of the responsibility for ensuring that any funds so allocated are applied in furtherance of such state's approved management program.

(g) The state shall be authorized to amend the management program. The modification shall be in accordance with the procedures required under subsection (c) of this section. Any amendment or modification of the program must be approved by the Secretary before additional administrative grants are made to the state under the program as amended.

(h) At the discretion of the state and with the approval of the Secretary, a management program may be developed and adopted in segments so that immediate attention may be devoted to those areas within the coastal zone which most urgently need management programs: *Provided,* That the state adequately provides for the ultimate coordination of the various segments of the management program into a single unified program and that the unified program will be completed as soon as is reasonably practicable.

INTERAGENCY COORDINATION AND COOPERATION

SEC. 307. (a) In carrying out his functions and responsibilities under this title, the Secretary shall consult with, cooperate with, and, to the maximum extent practicable, coordinate his activities with other interested Federal agencies.

(b) The Secretary shall not approve the management program submitted by a state pursuant to section 306 unless the views of Federal agencies principally affected by such program have been adequately considered. In case of serious disagreement between any Federal agency and the state in the development of the program the Secretary, in cooperation with the Executive Office of the President, shall seek to mediate the differences.

(c) (1) Each Federal agency conducting or supporting activities directly affecting the coastal zone shall conduct or support those activities in a manner which is, to the maximum extent practicable, consistent with approved state management programs.

(2) Any Federal agency which shall undertake any development project in the coastal zone of a state shall insure that the project is, to the maximum extent practicable, consistent with approved state management programs.

(3) After final approval by the Secretary of a state's management program, any applicant for a required Federal license or permit to conduct an activity affecting land or water uses in the coastal zone of that state shall provide in the application to the licensing or permitting agency a certification that the proposed activity complies with the state's approved program and that such activity will be conducted in a manner consistent with the program. At the same time, the applicant shall furnish to the state or its designated agency a copy of the certification, with all necessary information and data. Each coastal state shall

establish procedures for public notice in the case of all such certifica-
tions and, to the extent it deems appropriate, procedures for public
hearings in connection therewith. At the earliest practicable time, the
state or its designated agency shall notify the Federal agency concerned that the state concurs with or objects to the applicant's
certification. If the state or its designated agency fails to furnish the required notification within six months after receipt of its copy of the applicant's certification, the state's concurrence with the certification
shall be conclusively presumed. No license or permit shall be granted
by the Federal agency until the state or its designated agency has con-
curred with the applicant's certification or until, by the state's failure
to act, the concurrence is conclusively presumed, unless the Secretary,
on his own initiative or upon appeal by the applicant, finds, after providing a reasonable opportunity for detailed comments from the
Federal agency involved and from the state, that the activity is consistent with the objectives of this title or is otherwise necessary in the interest of national security.

(d) State and local governments submitting applications for Federal
assistance under other Federal programs affecting the coastal zone
shall indicate the views of the appropriate state or local agency as to
the relationship of such activities to the approved management program for the coastal zone. Such applications shall be submitted and
coordinated in accordance with the provisions of title IV of the Intergovernmental Coordination Act of 1968 (82 Stat. 1098). Federal
agencies shall not approve proposed projects that are inconsistent with
a coastal state's management program, except upon a finding by the
Secretary that such project is consistent with the purposes of this title
or necessary in the interest of national security.

(e) Nothing in this title shall be construed—

(1) to diminish either Federal or state jurisdiction, responsibility,
or rights in the field of planning, development, or control of water
resources, submerged lands, or navigable waters; nor to displace,
supersede, limit, or modify any interstate compact or the jurisdiction or responsibility of any legally established joint or common
agency of two or more states or of two or more states and the
Federal Government; nor to limit the authority of Congress to
authorize and fund projects;

(2) as superseding, modifying, or repealing existing laws applicable to the various Federal agencies; nor to affect the jurisdiction,

powers, or prerogatives of the International Joint Commission, United States and Canada, the Permanent Engineering Board, and the United States operating entity or entities established pursuant to the Columbia River Basin Treaty, signed at Washington, January 17, 1961, or the International Boundary and Water Commission, United States and Mexico.

(f) Notwithstanding any other provision of this title, nothing in this title shall in any way affect any requirement (1) established by the Federal Water Pollution Control Act, as amended, or the Clean Air Act, as amended, or (2) established by the Federal Government or by any state or local government pursuant to such Acts. Such requirements shall be incorporated in any program developed pursuant to this title and shall be the water pollution control and air pollution control requirements applicable to such program.

(g) When any state's coastal zone management program, submitted for approval or proposed for modification pursuant to section 306 of this title, includes requirements as to shorelands which also would be subject to any Federally supported national land use program which may be hereafter enacted, the Secretary, prior to approving such program, shall obtain the concurrence of the Secretary of the Interior, or such other Federal official as may be designated to administer the national land use program, with respect to that portion of the coastal zone management program affecting such inland areas.

PUBLIC HEARINGS

SEC. 308. All public hearings required under this title must be announced at least thirty days prior to the hearing date. At the time of the announcement, all agency materials pertinent to the hearings, including documents, studies, and other data, must be made available to the public for review and study. As similar materials are subsequently developed, they shall be made available to the public as they become available to the agency.

REVIEW OF PERFORMANCE

SEC. 309. (a) The Secretary shall conduct a continuing review of the management programs of the coastal states and of the performance of each state.

(b) The Secretary shall have the authority to terminate any financial assistance extended under section 306 and to withdraw any unexpended portion of such assistance if (1) he determines that the state is failing to adhere to and is not justified in deviating from the program approved by the Secretary; and (2) the state has been given notice of the proposed termination and withdrawal and given an opportunity to present evidence of adherence or justification for altering its program.

RECORDS

SEC. 310. (a) Each recipient of a grant under this title shall keep such records as the Secretary shall prescribe, including records which fully disclose the amount and disposition of the funds received under the grant, the total cost of the project or undertaking supplied by other sources, and such other records as will facilitate an effective audit.

(b) The Secretary and the Comptroller General of the United States, or any of their duly authorized representatives, shall have access for the purpose of audit and examination to any books, documents, papers, and records of the recipient of the grant that are pertinent to the determination that funds granted are used in accordance with this title.

ADVISORY COMMITTEE

SEC. 311. (a) The Secretary is authorized and directed to establish a Coastal Zone Management Advisory Committee to advise, consult with and make recommendations to the Secretary on matters of policy concerning the coastal zone. Such committee shall be composed of not more than fifteen persons designated by the Secretary and shall perform such functions and operate in such a manner as the Secretary may direct. The Secretary shall insure that the committee membership as a group possesses a broad range of experience and knowledge relating to problems involving management, use, conservation, protection, and development of coastal zone resources.

(b) Members of the committee who are not regular full-time employees of the United States, while serving on the business of the committee, including traveltime, may receive compensation at rates not exceeding $100 per diem; and while so serving away from their homes or regular places of business may be allowed travel expenses, including per diem in lieu of subsistence, as authorized by section 5703 of title 5, United States Code, for individuals in the Government service employed intermittently.

ESTUARINE SANCTUARIES

SEC. 312. The Secretary, in accordance with rules and regulations promulgated by him, is authorized to make available to a coastal state grants of up to 50 per centum of the costs of acquisition, development, and operation of estuarine sanctuaries for the purpose of creating natural field laboratories to gather data and make studies of the natural and human processes occurring within the estuaries of the coastal zone. The Federal share of the cost for each such sanctuary shall not exceed $2,000,000. No Federal funds received pursuant to section 305 or section 306 shall be used for the purpose of this section.

ANNUAL REPORT

SEC. 313. (a) The Secretary shall prepare and submit to the President for transmittal to the Congress not later than November 1 of each year a report on the administration of this title for the preceding fiscal year. The report shall include but not be restricted to (1) an identification of the state programs approved pursuant to this title during the preceding Federal fiscal year and a description of those programs; (2) a listing of the states participating in the provisions of this title and a description of the status of each state's programs and its accomplishments during the preceding Federal fiscal year; (3) an itemization of the allocation of funds to the various coastal states and a breakdown of the major projects and areas on which these funds were expended; (4) an identification of any state programs which ave been reviewed and disapproved or with respect to which grants have been terminated under this title, and a statement of the reasons for such action; (5) a listing of all activities and projects which, pursuant to the provisions of subsection (c) or subsection (d) of section 307, are not consistent with an applicable approved state management program; (6) a summary of the regulations issued by the Secretary or in effect during the preceding Federal fiscal year; (7) a summary of a coordinated national strategy and program for the Nation's coastal zone including identification and discussion of Federal, regional, state, and local responsibilities and functions therein; (8) a summary of outstanding problems arising in the administration of this title in order of priority; and (9) such other information as may be appropriate.

(b) The report required by subsection (a) shall contain such recommendations for additional legislation as the Secretary deems necessary to achieve the objectives of this title and enhance its effective operation.

RULES AND REGULATIONS

SEC. 314. The Secretary shall develop and promulgate, pursuant to section 553 of title 5, United States Code, after notice and opportunity for full participation by relevant Federal agencies, state agencies, local governments, regional organizations, port authorities, and other interested parties, both public and private, such rules and regulations as may be necessary to carry out the provisions of this title.

AUTHORIZATION OF APPROPRIATIONS

SEC. 315. (1) There are authorized to be appropriated—

(1) the sum of $9,000,000 for the fiscal year ending June 30, 1973, and for each of the fiscal years 1974 through 1977 for grants under section 305, to remain available until expended;

(2) such sums, not to exceed $30,000,000, for the fiscal year ending June 30, 1974, and for each of the fiscal years 1975 through 1977, as may be necessary, for grants under section 306 to remain available until expended; and

(3) such sums, not to exceed $6,000,000 for the fiscal year ending June 30, 1974, as may be necessary, for grants under section 312, to remain available until expended.

(b) There are also authorized to be appropriated such sums, not to exceed $3,000,000, for fiscal year 1973 and for each of the four succeeding fiscal years, as may be necessary for administrative expenses incident to the administration of this title.

Approved October 27, 1972.

Appendix D

New Jersey Coastal Area Facility Review Act

BE IT ENACTED by the Senate and General Assembly of the State of New Jersey:

1. This act shall be known and may be cited as the "Coastal Area *Facility* Review Act."

2. The Legislature finds and declares that New Jersey's bays, harbors, sounds, wetlands, inlets, the tidal portions of fresh, saline or partially saline streams and tributaries and their adjoining upland fastland drainage area nets, channels, estuaries, barrier beaches, near shore waters and intertidal areas together constitute an exceptional, unique, irreplaceable and delicately balanced physical, chemical and biologically acting and interacting natural environmental resource called the coastal area, that certain portions of the coastal area are now suffering serious adverse environmental effects resulting from existing facility activity impacts that would preclude or tend to preclude those multiple uses which support diversity and are in the best long-term, social, economic, aesthetic and recreational interests of all people of the State; and that, therefore, it is in the interest of the people of the State that all of the coastal area should be dedicated to those kinds of land uses which promote the public health, safety and welfare, protect public and private property, and are reasonably consistent and compatible with the natural laws governing the physical, chemical and biological environment of the coastal area.

It is further declared that the coastal area and the State will suffer continuing and ever-accelerating serious adverse economic, social and aesthetic effects unless the State assists, in accordance with the pro-

visions of this act, in the assessment of impacts, stemming from the future location and kinds of facilities within the coastal area, on the delicately balanced environment of that area.

The Legislature further recognizes the legitimate economic aspirations of the inhabitants of the coastal area and wishes to encourage the development of compatible land uses in order to improve the overall economic position of the inhabitants of that area within the framework of a comprehensive environmental design strategy which preserves the most ecologically sensitive and fragile area from inappropriate development and provides adequate environmental safeguards for the construction of any facilities in the coastal area. *

3. For the purposes of this act, unless the context clearly requires a different meaning, the following words shall have the following meanings:

a. "Commissioner" means the State Commissioner of Environmental Protection.

b. "Department" means the State Department of Environmental Protection.

c. *"*Facility*"* * includes any of the facilities designed or utilized for the following purposes:

(1) Electric power generation——
Oil, gas, or coal fired or any combination thereof.
Nuclear facilities.

(2) Food and food byproduct——
Beer, whiskey and wine production.
Fish processing, including the production of fish meal and fish oil.
Slaughtering, blanching, cooking, curing, and pickling of meats and poultry.
Trimming, culling, juicing, and blanching of fruits and vegetables.
Animal matter rendering plants.
Operations directly related to the production of leather or furs such as, but not limited to, unhairing, soaking, deliming, baiting, and tanning.

Curing and pickling of fruits and vegetables.

Pasteurization, homogenization, condensation, and evaporation of milk and cream to produce cheeses, sour milk, and related products.

Coffee bean and cocoa bean roasting.

(3) Incineration wastes——
Municipal wastes (larger than or equal to 50 tons per day).
Automobile body (20 automobiles per hour or larger).

(4) Paper production——
Pulp mills.
Paper mills.
Paperboard mills.
Building paper mills.
Building board mills.

(5) Public facilities *and housing*——
Sanitary landfills.
Waste treatment plants (sanitary sewage).
Road, airport, or highway construction.
New housing developments of 25 or more dwelling units or equivalent.
Expansion of existing developments *by the addition* of 25 or more dwelling units or equivalent.

(6) Agri-chemical production——
Pesticides manufacture and formulation operations or either thereof.
Superphosphate animal feed supplement manufacture.
Production of normal superphosphate.
Production of triple superphosphate.
Production of diammonium phosphate.

(7) Inorganic acids and salts manufacture——
Hydrofluoric acid and common salts.
Hydrochloric acid and common salts.
Nitric acid and common salts.
Sulfuric acid and common salts.
Phosphoric acid and common salts.
Chromic acid, including chromate and dichromate salts.

(8) Mineral products——

Asphalt batching and roofing operations including the preparation of bituminous concrete and concrete.

Cement production, including Portland, natural, masonry, and pozzolan cements.

Coal cleaning.

Clay, clay mining, and fly-ash sintering.

Calcium carbide production.

Stone, rock, gravel, and sand quarrying and processing.

Frit and glass production.

Fiberglass production.

Slag, rock and glass wool production (mineral wool).

Lime production, including quarrying.

Gypsum production, including quarrying.

Perlite manufacturing, including quarrying.

Asbestos fiber production.

(9) Chemical processes——

Ammonia manufacture.

Chlorine manufacture.

Caustic soda production.

Carbon black and charcoal production, including channel, furnace, and thermal processes.

Varnish, paint, lacquer, enamel, organic solvent, and inorganic or organic pigment manufacturing or formulating.

Synthetic resins or plastics manufacture including, but not limited to, alkyd resins, polyethylene, fluorocarbons, polypropylene, and polyvinylchloride.

Sodium carbonate manufacture.

Synthetic fibers production including, but not limited to, semi-synthetics such as viscose, rayon, and acetate, and true synthetics such as, but not limited to, nylon, orlon, and dacron, and the dyeing of these semi and true synthetics.

Synthetic rubber manufacture, including but not limited to, butadiene and styrene copolymers, and the reclamation of synthetic or natural rubbers.

The production of high and low explosives such as, but not limited to, TNT and nitrocellulose.

Soap and detergent manufacturing, including but not limited to, those synthetic detergents prepared from fatty alcohols or linear alkylate.

Elemental sulfur recovery plants not on the premises where petroleum refining occurs.

Used motor or other oil or related petroleum product reclamation operations.

Petroleum refining, including but not limited to, distillation, cracking, reforming, treating, blending, polymerization, isomerization, alkylation, and elemental sulfur recovery operations.

Organic dye and dye intermediate manufacturing.

Hydrogen cyanide or cyanide salts manufacture or use.

Glue manufacturing operations.

Manufacturing, fabricating, or processing medicinal and pharmaceutical products including the grading, grinding, or milling of botanicals.

(10) Storage——
Bulk storage, handling, and transfer facilities for crude oil*, gas* and finished petroleum products not on the premises where petroleum refining occurs.

Bulk storage, handling, transfer and manufacturing facilities of gas manufactured from inorganic and organic materials including coal gas, coke oven gas, water gas, producer, and oil gases.

(11) Metallurgical processes——
Production of aluminum oxide and aluminum metal and all common alloys, such as those with copper, magnesium, and silicon.

Production of titanium metal, salts, and oxides.

Metallurgical coke, petroleum coke, and byproduct coke manufacturing.

Copper, lead, zinc, and magnesium smelting and processing.

Ferroalloys manufacture such as, but not limited to, those combined with silicon, calcium, manganese and chrome.

Integrated steel and iron mill operations including, but not limited to, open hearth, basic oxygen, electric furnace, sinter plant, and rolling, drawing, and extruding operations.

Melting, smelting, refining, and alloying of scrap or other substances to produce brass and bronze ingots.

Gray iron foundry operations.

Steel foundry operations.

Beryllium metal or alloy production, including rolling, drawing and extruding operations.

Operations involving silver, arsenic, cadmium, copper, mercury, lead, nickel, chromium, and zinc including, but not limited to, production, recovery from scrap or salvage, alloy production, salt formation, electroplating, anodizing, and metallo-organics compound products preparation.

Stripping of oxides from and the cleaning of metals prior to plating, anodizing, or painting.

(12) Miscellaneous——

Operatings involving the scouring, desizing, cleaning, bleaching, and dyeing of wool.

Wood preserving processes which use coal or petroleum based products such as, but not limited to, coal tars and/or creosotes.

Manufacture, use, or distillation of phenols, cresols, or coal tar materials.

Manufacture of lead acid storage batteries and/or storage batteries produced from other heavy metals, such as nickel or cadmium.

Installation of above or underground pipelines designed to transport petroleum, natural gas, and sanitary sewage.

Operations involving the dyeing, bleaching, coating, impregnating, or glazing of paper.

Dyeing, bleaching, and printing of textiles other than wool. Chemical finishing for water repelling, fire resistance, and mildew proofing, including preshrinking, coating and impregnating.

Sawmill and planing mill operations.

Marine terminal and cargo handling facilities.

d. "Person" means and shall include corporations, companies, associations, societies, firms, partnerships and joint stock companies as well as individuals and governmental agencies.

e. "Governmental agencies" means the Government of the United States, the State of New Jersey, or any other states, their political subdivisions, agencies, or instrumentalities thereof, and interstate agencies.

4. The "coastal area" shall consist of all that certain area lying

between the line as hereinafter described and the line formed by the State's *seaward (Raritan Bay and Atlantic ocean) territorial jurisdiction on the east thereof, the State's bayward (Delaware Bay) territorial jurisdiction on the south and southwest thereof, and the State's riverward (Delaware River) territorial jurisdiction on the west thereto.* ***Beginning at the confluence of Cheesequake Creek with the Raritan Bay; thence southwesterly along the center line of Cheesequake Creek to its intersection with the Garden State Parkway;**** then southeasterly along the Garden State Parkway to Exit 117 at State Highway 36; thence northeasterly along State Highway 36 to the intersection of Middle Road (County 516); thence easterly along Middle Road to the intersection of Palmer Avenue (County 7); thence northeasterly on Main Street to the intersection of State Highway 36; thence easterly on State Highway 36 to the intersection of Navesink Avenue; thence southerly on Navesink Avenue to the intersection of Monmouth Avenue at Navesink; thence westerly on Monmouth Avenue to its intersection with Browns Dock Road; thence southerly on Browns Dock Road to its intersection with Cooper Road; thence southwesterly on Cooper Road to the intersection of State Highway 35; thence southerly on State Highway 35 to its intersection with State Highway 71; thence southeasterly on State Highway 71 to its crossing of the Central Railroad of New Jersey tracks; thence southerly along the Central Railroad of New Jersey tracks to its intersection of 6th Avenue (County 2); thence westerly on 6th Avenue (County 2) to the intersection of State Highway 33; thence westerly along State Highway 33 to the crossing of State Highway 18; thence southerly on State Highway 18 to its intersection of Marconi Road; thence southeasterly on Marconi Road to Adrienne Road, continuing south on Adrienne Road to Belmar Boulevard; thence easterly on Belmar Boulevard and 16th Avenue to the intersection of State Highway 71; thence southerly on State Highway 71 to the intersection of State Highway 35; thence northwesterly along State Highway 35 to State Highway 34 at the Brielle Circle; thence northwesterly along State Highway 34 to the Garden State Parkway at Exit 96; thence southwesterly along the Garden State Parkway to the intersection of the Monmouth, Ocean County boundary; thence westerly along said boundary to the intersection of the Central Railroad of New Jersey tracks; thence southwesterly* along the tracks of the Central Railroad of New Jersey to its junction with the tracks of the Pennsylvania Railroad near Whiting; thence easterly along the tracks of the Pennsylvania Railroad to its intersection with the Garden State Parkway near South Toms River; thence southerly along the Garden State Parkway to its intersection with County Road 539 at Garden State Parkway exit 58; thence northerly along County Road 539 to its intersection with Martha-Stafford Forge Road; thence westerly along Martha-Stafford Forge Road to its intersection with Spur 563; thence northerly along Spur 563 to its intersection with County Road 563; thence southerly along County Road 563 to its intersection with County Road 542 at Green Bank; thence northwesterly along County Road 542 to its intersection with Weekstown-Pleasant Mills Road; thence southeasterly along Weekstown-Pleasant Mills Road to its intersection with County Road 563 at Weekstown; thence southeasterly along County Road 563 to its intersection with Clarks Landing Road leading to Port Republic; thence easterly along Clarks Landing Road to its intersection with the Garden State Parkway; thence southerly along the Garden State Parkway to its intersection with Alt. 559, and thence northwesterly along Alt. 559 to its intersection with ****County Road 559 at Gravelly Run; thence northwesterly along County Road 559 to its intersection with U.S. 40 and S.R. 50 at Mays Landing; thence westerly along combined U.S. 40 and S.R. 50 to its intersection with S.R. 50;**** thence southerly on S.R. 50 to its intersection with ****Buck Hill Road near Buck Hill; thence westerly along Buck Hill (River Road) Road to its intersection with S.R. 49; thence southeasterly along S.R. 49 to its intersection with S.R. 50; thence southeasterly along S.R. 50 to its intersection with County Road 585; thence southwesterly along County Road 585 to its intersection with S.R. 47 at Dennisville;**** thence northwesterly along S.R. 47 to its intersection with ****State Road 49 at Millville; thence through Millville along State Road 49 to its inter-Road 555 to its intersection with County Road 27; thence southerly along County 27 to its intersection with County Road 70; thence southerly on County Road 70 to Center of**** Mauricetown; thence through Mauricetown westerly on County Road 548 to its intersection with the tracks of the Central Railroad of New Jersey; thence northwesterly on the tracks of the Central Railroad of New Jersey to its intersection with County Road 98; thence ****easterly along County Road 98 to the intersection with County Road 38; thence northerly along County Road 38 to its intersection with S.R. 49 east of Bridgeton; thence westerly along S.R. 49 through Bridgeton to its intersection with County Road 5

(Roadstown Road); thence westerly along County Road 5 (Roadstown Road) to Roadstown; thence northwesterly along the Roadstown Road to County Road 47; thence southwesterly along County Road 47 to its intersection with County Road 19; thence along County Road 19 northwesterly to Gum Tree Corner; thence northwesterly along County Road 19 from Gum Tree Corner across Stowe Creek to its intersection with Salem County Road 59 (Hancock's Bridge Road); thence northwesterly along County Road 59 to its intersection with County Road 51 at Coopers Branch; thence northeasterly along County Road 51 to its intersection with S.R. 49 at Quinton; thence northwesterly along S.R. 49 to its intersection with County Road 50; thence southwesterly along County Road 50 to its intersection with County Road 58; thence southerly on County Road 58 to its intersection with County Road 24; thence westerly along County Road 24 to its intersection with County Road 65; thence northerly along County Road 65 (Walnut Street) to its intersection with County Road 4; thence westerly along County Road 4 and northerly along County Road 4 and thence easterly along County Road 4 to its intersection with State Road 49; thence northerly along State Road 49 (Front Street) to its intersection with County Road 57; thence easterly along County Road 57 to its intersection with State Road 45; thence northerly along State Road 45 to its intersection County Road 540 at Pointers; thence northerly and northwesterly along County Road 540 (Deepwater-Slapes Corner Road) to its intersection with the New Jersey Turnpike; thence westerly along the New Jersey Turnpike to its intersection with County Road 33; thence southerly along County Road 33 to its intersection with State Road 49; thence southeasterly along S.R. 49 to its intersection with County Road 26; thence northwesterly along County Road 26 to the Killcohook National Wildlife Refuge; thence northwesterly along this northeasterly boundary to the limits of the State's territorial jurisdiction on the Delaware River; provided, however, that the coastal area shall not include all that certain area in Cape May County lying within a line beginning at the intersection of S.R. 47 and County Road 54; thence westerly on County westerly on County Road 54; to the intersection of County Road 3; thence southeasterly on County Road 3 through the intersection of County Road 3 with County Road 13 to the intersection with County Road 47; thence easterly and northerly along County Road 47 to its intersection with State Road 9; thence on County Road 54; to the intersection of County Road 3; thence southeasterly on

County Road 3 through the intersection of County Road 3 with County Road 13 to the intersection with County Road 47; thence easterly and northerly along County Road 47 to its intersection with State Road 9; thence northerly along State Road 9 to its intersection with State Road 47; thence westerly along State Road 47 to its intersection with County Road 54.* * *

* * **5. No person shall construct or cause to be constructed a facility in the coastal area until he has applied for and received a permit issued by the Commissioner; however, the provisions of this act shall not apply to facilities for which on-site construction, including site preparation, was in process on or prior to the effective date of this act.* * **

6. Any person proposing to construct or cause to be constructed *a facility in the coastal area* shall file an application for a permit with the commissioner, in such form and with such information as the commissioner may prescribe. The application shall include an environmental impact statement as described in this act.

7. The environmental impact statement shall provide the information needed to evaluate the effects of a proposed project upon the environment of the coastal area.

The statement shall include:

a. An inventory of existing environmental conditions at the project site and in the surrounding region which shall describe air quality, water quality, water supply, hydrology, geology, soils, topography, vegetation, wildlife, aquatic organisms, ecology, demography, land use, aesthetics, history, and archeology; *for housing, the inventory shall describe water quality, water supply, hydrology, geology, soils and topography;*

b. A project description shall specify what is to be done and how it is to be done, during construction and operation;

c. A listing of all licenses, permits or other approvals as required by law and the status of each;

d. An assessment of the probable impact of the project upon all topics described in a.;

e. A listing of adverse environmental impacts which cannot be avoided;

f. Steps to be taken to minimize adverse environmental impacts during construction and operation, both at the project site and in the surrounding region;

g. Alternatives to all or any part of the project with reasons for their acceptability or nonacceptability;

h. A reference list of pertinent published information relating to the project, the project site, and the surrounding region.

8. a. Within 30 days following receipt of an application, the commissioner shall notify the applicant in writing regarding its completeness. The commissioner may declare the application to be complete for filing or may notify the applicant of specific deficiencies. The commissioner, within 15 days following the receipt of additional information to correct deficiencies, shall notify the applicant of the completeness of the amended application. The application shall not be considered to be filed until it has been declared complete by the commissioner.

b. The commissioner, within *15* days of declaring the application complete for filing, shall set a date for the hearing. The date for the hearing shall be set not later than *60* days after the application is declared complete for filing.

9. *a.* The commissioner, or a member of the department designated by him, shall hold a hearing to afford interested parties standing and the opportunity to present, orally or in writing, both their position concerning the application and any data they may have developed in reference to the environmental affects of the proposed facility.

b. The commissioner, within 15 days after the hearing, may require an applicant to submit any additional information necessary for the complete review of the application.

10. The commissioner shall review filed applications, including the environmental impact statement and all information presented at public hearings. He shall issue a permit only if he finds that the proposed facility:

a. Conforms with all applicable air, water and radiation emission and effluent standards and all applicable water quality criteria and air quality standards.

b. *Prevents air* emissions and water effluents *in excess of* the existing dilution, assimilative, and recovery capacities of the air and water environments at the site and within the surrounding region.

c. Provides for the handling and disposal of litter, trash, and refuse in such a manner as to minimize adverse environmental effects and the threat to the public health, safety, and welfare.

d. Would result in minimal feasible impairment of the regenerative capacity of water aquifers or other ground or surface water supplies.

e. Would cause minimal feasible interference with the natural functioning of plant, animal, fish, and human life processes at the site and within the surrounding region.

f. Is located or constructed so as to neither endanger human life or property nor otherwise impair the public health, safety, and welfare.

g. Would result in minimal practicable degradation of unique or irreplaceable land types, historical or archeological areas, and existing scenic and aesthetic attributes at the site and within the surrounding region.

11. *Notwithstanding the applicant's compliance with the criteria listed in section 10 of this act, if* the commissioner finds that the proposed facility would violate or tend to violate the *purpose and intent of this act as specified in section 2, or if the commissioner finds that the proposed facility would materially contribute to an already serious and unacceptable level of environmental degradation or resource exhaustion,* he may *deny the permit application, or he may issue a permit subject to such conditions as he finds reasonably necessary to promote the public health, safety and* welfare, to protect public and private property, wildlife and marine fisheries, and to preserve, protect and enhance the natural environment. ****In addition, the construction and operation of a nuclear electricity generating facility shall not be approved by the commissioner unless he shall find that the proposed method for disposal of radioactive waste material to be produced or generated by such facility will be safe, conforms to standards established by the Atomic Energy Commission and will effectively remove danger to life and the environment from such waste material.****

12. The commissioner shall notify the applicant within *60* days after the hearing as to the granting or denial of a permit. The reasons for granting or denying the permit shall be stated. In the event the commissioner required additional information as provided for in section

9, he shall notify the applicant of his decision within 90 days following the receipt of the information.

13. There is hereby created the Coastal Area Review Board, in but not of the Department of Environmental Protection, which shall consist of three voting members who shall be the Commissioner of Environmental Protection or his designated representative, the Commissioner of Labor and Industry or his designated representative and the Commissioner of Community Affairs or his designated representative. No vote on a permit request shall be taken unless all voting members are present.

*The Coastal Area Review Board shall have the power to hear appeals from decisions of the commissioner pursuant to section 12. The board may affirm or reverse the decision of the commissioner with respect to applicability of any provision of this act to a proposed use; it may modify any permit granted by the commissioner, grant a permit denied by him, deny a permit granted by him, or confirm his grant of a permit. The board shall review filed applications, including the environmental impact statement and all information presented at public hearings and any other information the commissioner makes available to the board prior to the affirmation or reversal of a decision of the commissioner. **

14. In the event of rental, lease, sale or other conveyances by an applicant to whom a permit is issued, such permit, with any conditions, shall be continued in force and shall apply to the new tenant, lessee, owner, or assignee so long as there is no change in the nature of the facility set forth in the original application.

15. The denial of an application shall in no way adversely affect the future submittal of a new application.

16. The commissioner shall, within 2 years of the taking effect of this act, prepare an environmental inventory of the environmental resources of the coastal area and of the existing facilities and land use developments within the coastal area and an estimate of the capability of the various area within the coastal area to absorb and react to man-made stresses. The commissioner shall, within 3 years of the taking effect of this act, develop from this environmental inventory alternate long-term environmental management strategies which take into account the paramount need for preserving environmental values and the legitimate need for economic and residential growth within the coastal area. The commissioner shall, within 4 years of the taking effect of this act, select from the alternate environmental management strategies an environmental design for the coastal area. The environmental design shall be the approved environmental management strategy for the coastal area and shall include a delineation of various areas appropriate for the development of residential and industrial facilities of various types, depending on the sensitivity and fragility of the adjacent environment to the existence of such facilities. The environmental inventory, the alternate long-term environmental management strategies and the environmental design for the coastal area shall be presented to the Governor and the Legislature within the time frame indicated herein.*

17. The department is hereby authorized to adopt, amend and repeal rules and regulations to effectuate the purposes of this act.

18. If any person violates any of the provisions of this act, rule, regulation or order promulgated or issued pursuant to the provisions of this act, the department may institute a civil action in the Superior Court for injunctive relief to prohibit and prevent such violation or violations and said court may proceed in a summary manner. Any person who violates any of the provisions of this act, rule, regulation or order promulgated or issued pursuant to this act shall be liable to a penalty of not more than $3,000.00 to be collected in a summary proceeding or in any case before a court of competent jurisdiction wherein injunctive relief has been requested. If the violation is of a continuing nature, each day during which it continues shall constitute an additional, separate and distinct offense. The department is hereby authorized and empowered to compromise and settle any claim for a penalty under this section in such amount in the discretion of the department as may appear appropriate and equitable under the circumstances.

19. The provisions of this act *shall not be regarded as to be in derogation of any powers now existing and* shall be regarded as supplemental and in addition to powers* conferred by other laws *including municipal zoning authority. The provisions of this act shall not apply to those portions of the coastal areas* *regulated pursuant to enforceable orders under the Wetlands Act, C. 13:9A-1 *et seq.*, *section 16 however shall apply to the entire area within the boundaries described herein.* *

*20. * This act shall be liberally construed to effectuate the purpose and intent thereof.

*21. * If any provision of this act or the application thereof to any person or circumstances is held invalid, the remainder of the act and the application of such provision to persons or circumstances other than those to which it is held invalid, shall not be affected thereby.

*22. * There is hereby appropriated to the Department of Environmental Protection for the purposes of this act the sum of $100,000.00.

23. This act shall take effect 90 days from the date of enactment, except that section 22 shall take effect immediately. *